Violence Against Women and Girls: Effectiveness of Intervention Programs

Gender Equality, Volume 3

Dr. Milos Kankaras

Published by Dr. Miloš Kankaraš, 2022.

While every precaution has been taken in the preparation of this book, the publisher assumes no responsibility for errors or omissions, or for damages resulting from the use of the information contained herein.

VIOLENCE AGAINST WOMEN AND GIRLS: EFFECTIVENESS OF INTERVENTION PROGRAMS

First edition. July 25, 2022.

ISBN: 979-8223478942

Written by Dr. Milos Kankaras.

Violence Against Women and Girls: Effectiveness of Intervention Programs

Dr Miloš Kankaraš

Executive summary

Violence against women and girls (VAWG) is a global health and wellbeing concern and a human rights violation. It is estimated that about one-third of women worldwide experience some form of VAWG at some point in their lives, with this proportion reaching two thirds in some countries (WHO, 2013). VAWG has severe detrimental consequences to its victims, including homicide, suicide, injuries, unintended pregnancies, mental health problems and other issues. VAWG also impacts the broader community, as affected women are less likely to participate in regular activities, have reduced capacity to care for themselves and their children, work, and use available economic opportunities (International Rescue Committee, 2012).

VAWG is preventable. That is why there has been increasing policy attention to this issue in recent years, resulting in a growing number of VAWG intervention programmes implemented worldwide. These programmes are also increasingly informed by the emerging academic and policy research on the causes, related factors and consequences of VAWG. VAWG intervention programs aim to reduce the risks of various forms of VAWG occurring or repeating and provide support to VAWG victims. However, developing and implementing an effective VAWG prevention intervention is not easy. It requires a good understanding of the nature of the problem, the cultural and socio-economic context in which it occurs, and the underlying drivers, risks and mitigating factors that affect the likelihood of VAWG occurrence.

The degree to which VAWG interventions achieve their aims is the question asked in impact evaluation studies empirically evaluating programme outcomes. They mostly do so by comparing target outcomes between the group that received the intervention and a control group using experimental and quasi-experimental methods. Impact evaluation studies are critical for gathering empirical evidence on what kind of interventions work, for whom, under which conditions, for which outcomes and through which mechanisms. Such empirical insights can then be used in future VAWG interventions to avoid inefficient approaches, build on identified positive aspects, fine-tune the methodological design and thus significantly improve chances for achieving desired positive change.

In this report, we provide a general overview of the globally available empirical evidence on the effectiveness of VAWG intervention programs. First, we describe the types of conducted VAWG programmes, their prevalence and their main characteristics. We then examine findings concerning the effectiveness of these interventions, summarised across different intervention approaches and different forms of VAWG. Finally, we analyse the quality and quantity of the reviewed empirical evidence on VAWG programmes' effectiveness and discuss some of the critical gaps identified in this evidence.

The report primarily focuses on the findings presented in several systematic reviews that evaluated results from impact evaluation studies on various forms of VAWG. The reviewed evidence is gathered in high-income countries (HIC) and low- and middle-income countries (LMIC). It is based on studies implementing experimental or quasi-experimental designs and systematically measuring their target outcomes. The evidence comprises studies on harmful traditional practices, intimate partner violence, non-partner sexual assaults, trafficking, child sexual abuse, and peer violence. Reviewed studies implement various intervention approaches, including individual-level interventions, group-based training, economic empowerment, community mobilisation, system-wide multi-component strategies, etc.

*The **main findings** of our review are the following:*

Few VAWG interventions employ robust impact assessment

Unfortunately, only a minority of VAWG programmes have incorporated robust systems to monitor and evaluate their impact, resulting in a relatively limited amount of available empirical evidence on their effectiveness. That might be due to many factors, such as the difficulty of obtaining reliable data, the complexity and context-specificity of VAWG interventions, and the political and social dynamics surrounding these issues. Nevertheless, by assessing impact and results, we have an opportunity to build a critical evidence base and to learn how change happens, contributing to overall efforts to prevent VAWG.

The number of impact assessment studies in the VAWG field is rapidly growing

One very encouraging development is that the evidence base has rapidly increased in recent years and is expected to expand further. That means that we can expect more solid evidence on what works and under which conditions over the coming decades.

Positive change through VAWG interventions is possible

Analysis of the effectiveness of VAWG interventions confirms that change is possible, i.e. occurring or reoccurring VAWG is preventable. However, the presented findings also point out that positive change is by no means guaranteed or even the most likely intervention outcome. In high-income countries, secondary interventions with the VAWG victims have often shown success in improving survivors' physical and mental health. On the other hand, evidence of their effectiveness in reducing the rates of revictimization is still weak. Considerable research has also been done about interventions designed to address perpetrators, but the evidence of their effectiveness is limited. In the LMIC context, the main focus of VAWG interventions is the prevention of various forms of violence. Assessment of these programmes indicates that it is possible to reduce the prevalence of violence, with some interventions reaching substantial positive effects within the timeframe of the programmes.

Most of the VAWG interventions have limited to no positive impact

*More robust evidence is dearly needed since the current evidence base is still relatively weak and inconclusive. The main, and probably most striking finding from this overview is that among selected VAWG interventions, more than two-thirds were found to have no effects on targeted outcomes (**Figure 1**). Half of the remaining interventions had mixed results. Only every tenth evaluated VAWG intervention had a significant positive impact! Furthermore, in 5% of cases, adverse effects of VAWG intervention are observed.*

Figure 1: Impact assessment across selected studies by type of violence

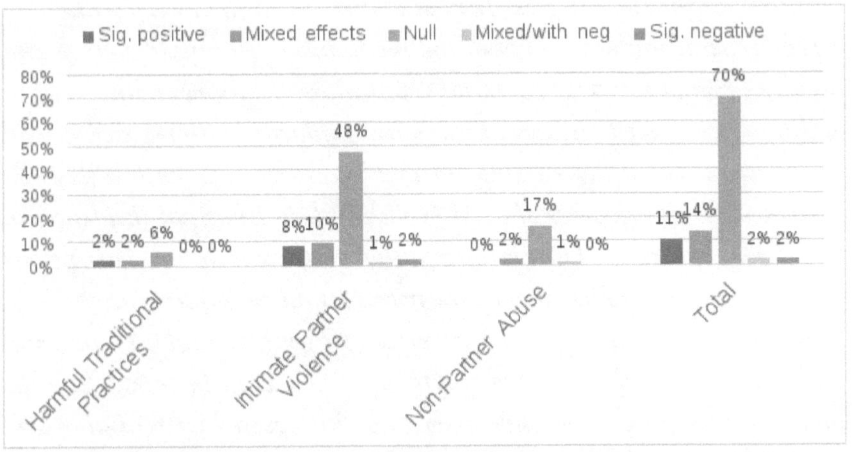

Source: *Adjusted from Arango et al. (2014). Interventions to prevent or reduce violence against women and girls: A systematic review of reviews. http://dx.doi.org/10.13140/ RG.2.1.2545.6168*

Some VAWG interventions have negative consequences

Unfortunately, findings suggest that some interventions have had unintended negative consequences on some outcomes. Although the proportion of such programmes was relatively small, such findings point out the need for careful planning of intervention programmes to minimise the risks of such events occurring. But they also indicate how important it is to conduct impact evaluations of all VAWG intervention programs to provide an opportunity for all practitioners and researchers in the VAWG field to learn what works and what doesn't and to use such knowledge in the future interventions.

The quality of available empirical evidence is generally poor

Unfortunately, the existing evidence on the effectiveness of VAWG programmes has several serious flaws and limitations that affect its quality and, consequently, its usability. Reviewed studies are characterised by limited consistency, rigour, and quality of employed evaluation processes, measures and methodologies. They also often based their intervention on a poor general understanding of the mechanism of targeted change and involved risk factors and potential moderators of intervention effects. In addition, the impact assessment was often conducted with relatively small sample sizes, not using reliable outcome measures, and with a focus on various indirect measures of VAWG rather than its actual incidences in the target population. Furthermore, although there is an increasing effort to evaluate programmes' impact, the teams conducting interventions often lack the skills, funding, and expertise to generate robust empirical evidence. As a result, obtained empirical results, even in cases where the impact was assessed as positive, have to be interpreted with caution and care, taking into account specific methodological constraints ingrained within each particular study design.

Evidence gaps are many

There are many critical gaps in existing empirical data on the effectiveness of VAWG interventions that severely limit the usability and generalisability of its findings. In the following paragraphs, we will outline some of the key evidence gaps in this area. 1) First of all, there is much less robust empirical research on the effectiveness of VAWG interventions coming from LMIC contexts. 2) There is a considerable difference in the amount of conducted studies across different research areas. Some areas, such as micro-finance interventions, receive much more attention than complex and multi-component programmes to transform system-level discrimination or change social norms. 3) Limited evidence exists on the effectiveness of intervention programmes with particularly vulnerable groups of women and girls, such as LGBT populations, people living with disabilities, chronic illness, people belonging to various ethnic or religious minorities, etc. 4) There is very little usable empirical evidence on VAWG intervention effectiveness coming from severely deprived or conflict regions. 5) Very few evaluations assessed the impact on VAWG beyond their respondent groups, at the broader community or population levels. 6) Most studies fail to measure their programmes' medium- and long-term outcomes. 7) Few interventions examine the mechanism through which change occurs or the influence of related risk factors. 8) Finally, only very few studies examined the cost-effectiveness or the optimal intensity of their interventions concerning the desired outcomes.

Evidence gaps are in key areas

Most of the identified evidence gaps are observed in those areas where such evidence would be most needed and valuable. For example, the regions with the highest prevalence of VAWG (South Asia, Middle East and North Africa, and Sub-Saharan Africa) have some of the lowest rates of good quality impact assessment studies. Likewise, women and girls belonging to vulnerable groups are at the same time more likely to experience VAWG and less likely to be part of the targeted VAWG intervention programme. Furthermore, VAWG tends to be substantially higher in conflict and post-conflict populations, yet we know the least about what works in these contexts. Such a situation means that those women and girls who need help the most tend to get it the least and that we know very little, if anything at all, about how to help them effectively.

Evidence gaps are preventing the scaling of good practices

Most of the critical information needed to build upon positive evidence, scale it up, and adapt it for use in broader contexts is not available. For example, most programmes do not measure impact across more general population categories, do not measure longer-term effects and lack information on the potential scalability of any given intervention to other similar or distinct contexts. In addition, there is little solid evidence on the mechanism of intervention and the process through which desired change could be generated and sustained, as testified in the widespread instances of "conflicting" evidence among the programmes implementing similar strategies. Surveyed reviews also indicate a great deal of heterogeneity between study outcomes. These outcomes vary not only across different intervention strategies and types of VAWG but also across the studies that utilise the same approach and target the same form of violence. In other cases, the effects of a particular intervention are unclear, with some outcomes positively influenced and not the others. In such a situation, it is challenging to extract a consistent and reliable set of empirical insights on "what works" in this area that could be used to improve the effectiveness of new VAWG interventions.

Key lessons learned

Nonetheless, a small but growing body of rigorously tested interventions demonstrates that preventing VAWG is possible and can achieve large effect sizes. The interventions with the most positive findings used multiple, well-integrated approaches and engaged with numerous stakeholders over more extended periods. They also addressed underlying risk factors for violence, including social norms regarding gender dynamics and the acceptability of violence and women's economic independence. Surveyed findings also indicate the need to employ an approach adequate to the given situation, cultural and socio-economic context and to engage key local stakeholders to give them a sense of agency and ownership of the programme's goals.

Moving forward, identified limitations in the quantity and quality of empirical evidence on "what works" and limited effectiveness of the VAWG interventions, in general, all point to the imperative of significantly increasing investment in the rigorous impact evaluation of VAWG programmes. These investments should especially prioritise research conducted in the areas with identified evidence gaps, including studies conducted in the LMIC contexts, with vulnerable populations, and in conflict areas. Furthermore, evaluation studies with crucial design characteristics that enable the potential scalability of their results should be prioritised. These features include a more comprehensive target population, more extended impact tracking, examination of mechanisms of change and related broader risk factors, and consideration of the intervention's scalability, sustainability, and cost-effectiveness.

Prevention of VAWG is possible but not easy to achieve. VAWG programmes have to be designed with the required expertise and knowledge, building upon the best available evidence and fully accounting for the complexity of issues at hand. Importantly, they have to be accompanied by a robust impact assessment design to evaluate their effectiveness accurately. Generation of such evidence would help build a much-needed knowledge base on what works and what doesn't. This area badly needs such knowledge to improve the effectiveness of its interventions with the ultimate aim of preventing VAWG from occurring or helping its victims in moments of need.

Abbreviations and acronyms

AA Alcoholics Anonymous

BIP Batterer intervention programmes

CAM Child abuse and maltreatment

CSA Child sexual abuse

CBO Community-based organisation

CBT Cognitive behavioural therapy

CM Child marriage

CPV Child peer violence

CSA Child Sexual Abuse

DFIDUK Department for International Development

FGM Female genital mutilation

FSW Female Sex Workers

GBV Gender-based violence

HIC High Income Countries

HTP Harmful traditional practices

ICT Information and communications technology

IPV Intimate partner violence

LMIC Low- and middle-income countries

NPSA Non-partner sexual assault

PSM Propensity score matching

RCT Randomised controlled trial

RDD Regression discontinuity design

SR Systematic review

VAWG Violence against women and girls

UN United Nations

WHO World Health Organization

1. Introduction

Some forty years ago, violence against women and girls (VAWG) was not an issue attracting much, if any, international attention. Most victims of VAWG suffered in silence, with little public concern or interest. Such a situation began to change in the 1980s, as women-rights groups started to organise locally and internationally to demand attention to the widespread prevalence of physical, sexual and psychological abuse and violence that affect many women and girls. Thanks mainly to the effort of these and aligned non-governmental groups, VAWG has gradually been reco gnised as a critical human rights issue of direct relevance to women's health and wellbeing.

With the international attention to the VAWG issue now secured, what is needed is methodologically rigorous research that will inform and guide the formulation and implementation of effective intervention programs and prevention strategies (Ellsberg et al., 2008). Unfortunately, until relatively recently, most empirical research in the domain of VAWG was based on anecdotal accounts or exploratory studies administered on non-representative samples (Ellsberg et al., 2008). However, over the last two decades, and especially in the previous ten years, many empirical studies in the VAWG area have been administered. Some of these studies have also evaluated their impact, offering clues about the effectiveness of various interventions in preventing different forms of VAWG.

This report aims to overview and synthesise existing empirical evidence from impact assessment studies that have evaluated intervention programs in the area of violence against women and girls (VAWG). Namely, this report tries to answer "what works" and "what doesn't work" in VAWG interventions, but also "what is still unknown" regarding the effectiveness of such interventions. The evidence is collected from high-income countries (HICs) and low- and middle-income countries (LMICs) across different VAWG categories and different types of interventions.

This report

Report objectives

The report is drafted with the following objectives:

- to provide an overview of the scope and content of existing empirical evidence on the effectiveness of VAWG interventions;

- to examine the quantity and quality of the available evidence;

- to outline the main limitations and gaps in the available empirical evidence;

- to provide recommendations for future work in this area.

Methodology

The report is based on the findings presented in various reviews and meta-analyses published in recent years, each of which summarized and, in some cases, evaluated whole or parts of empirical evidence in this area. The report aims to present a comprehensive overview of the evidence, including relevant findings from the entire selected literature. Consequently, the evidence we reviewed is more extensive than in any of the reviewed papers and reports. We prioritised compiling evidence from experimental (i.e. randomised controlled trials – RCTs) and quasi-experimental designs. However, we also included a few studies with other designs, reviewed in some selected meta-analyses. Given that overviews provided in different reviews differently categorized their findings, we decided to present primary empirical evidence using two main types of such categorisations: by type of VAWG and by type of interventions.

Report structure

After shortly outlining the primary forms, prevalence and consequences of VAWG in the remainder of the introductory chapter, in chapter 2, we will present some of the principal characteristics of VAWG interventions. Then, in chapter 3, we will present key empirical findings on the effectiveness of these interventions, followed by the evaluation of limitations and gaps in presented empirical evidence in chapter 4. Finally, the report finishes with chapter 5, in which we offer a concluding discussion and the report's summary.

Forms and prevalence of violence against women and girls

"Violence against Women and Girls" (VAWG) represents any act of gender-based violence that results in or is likely to result in physical, sexual, or psychological harm or suffering to women or girls. It includes threats of such acts, coercion, or arbitrary deprivation of liberty, whether in public or private life. VAWG is the most widespread form of abuse worldwide, affecting one-third of all women in their lifetime (WHO, 2013). It is a violation of fundamental human rights and a drag on development. Thus, addressing violence against women and girls is a central development goal in its own right and key to achieving other development outcomes for individual women, their families, communities and nations.

VAWG takes many forms, including sexual, physical, and psychological abuse. It occurs in the home, on the streets, in schools, workplaces, farm fields, and in refugee camps, during times of peace and especially during conflicts and crises. Intimate partner violence (IPV) is one of the most common forms of VAWG (**Figure 2**). It refers to acts and behaviour of the current or previous husband, boyfriend, or another partner that causes physical, sexual or psychological harm. It includes physical aggression, sexual coercion, psychological abuse and controlling behaviours. Such violence both reflects and reinforces underlying gender-based inequalities.

Figure 2: Prevalence of intimate partner violence (IPV) around the world

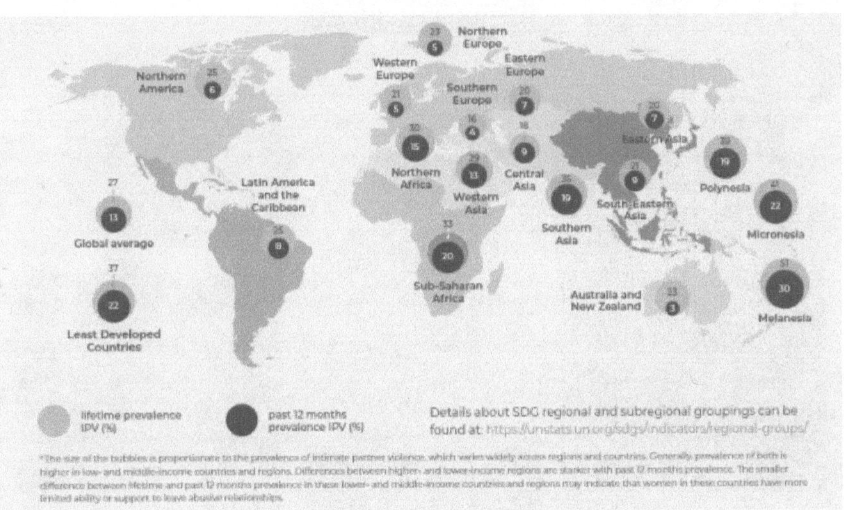

Source: WHO (2018). Global Fact Sheet. Violence Against Women: Prevalence Estimates[1], 2018.

Forms of VAWG can also be distinguished according to the age or life stage during which it occurs, indicating the specific risks and experiences of women and girls living under conditions of violence and

---

1. https://apps.who.int/iris/rest/bitstreams/1349966/retrieve

insecurity (Solotaroff and Pande, 2014). Different forms of violence or abuse can occur throughout the lives of women and girls, starting at the prenatal period, through infancy, childhood, adolescence, youth, reproductive age, and later in life (Gennari, 2014). That is why it is essential to adopt a lifecycle approach in addressing VAWG at all places and in all women's and girls' phases in life. The main types of violence women and girls experience during different life phases are presented in **Figure 3** below.

Figure 3: Forms of Violence Against Women and Girls by Life Cycle Stages

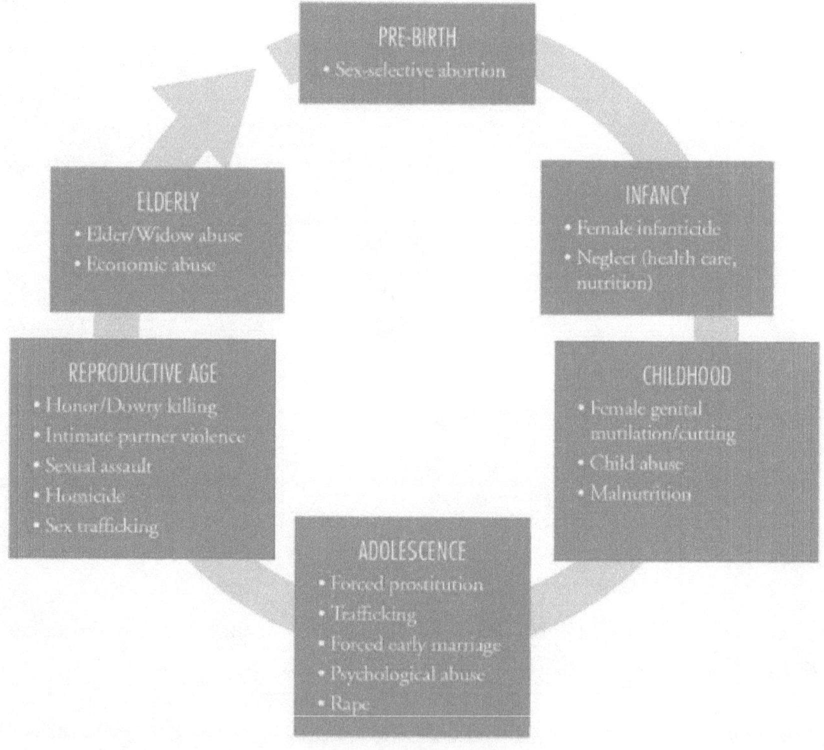

Source: Adapted from Watts and Zimmerman (2002) and Shane and Ellsberg (2002)

Definitions of the primary forms of VAWG that we will discuss in this report are outlined in **Table 1**.

Table 1: Forms of VAWG and their definitions

Child abuse or maltreatment	Child abuse or maltreatment constitutes all forms of physical and emotional ill-treatment, sexual abuse, neglect, negligent treatment, commercial or other exploitation. Such abuse can result in actual or potential harm to the child's health, survival, development, or dignity in the context of a relationship of responsibility, trust or power (WHO, 1999).
Child sexual abuse	Child sexual abuse, more specifically, includes contacts or interactions between a child and an older or more knowledgeable child or adult who uses the child as an object of gratification for their own needs. These contacts or interactions are carried out against the child using force, trickery, bribes, threats or pressure (UNICEF, 2001).
Intimate partner violence	IPV refers to any behaviour in an intimate relationship that causes physical, sexual, or psychological harm, including aggression, sexual coercion, psychological abuse and controlling behaviour (WHO, 2005). An intimate partner is a person with whom an individual has a close, personal relationship characterized by emotional connectedness, regular contact or sexual behaviour, identification as a couple, and cohabitation. Intimate partners may include current or former spouses, boyfriends or girlfriends, dating partners, and ongoing sexual partners (Breiding et al., 2015).
Sexual violence – partner or non-partner	Any action in which one person uses force, coercion or psychological intimidation to force another to carry out a sexual act against their will or participate in unwanted sexual relations (WHO, 2004). When carried out by a current or previous husband, partner or boyfriend, this is intimate partner

	sexual violence (IPV), and when performed by someone else, is non-partner sexual violence.
Harmful traditional practices	Any incident of violence perpetrated in the name of social, cultural or religious values. It includes female genital mutilation/cutting and child marriage.
Human trafficking	Violence experienced by someone recruited or harboured by another person through the use of force and for exploitation.
Peer violence	Repeated acts of physical or verbal violence (verbal abuse or name-calling). Many measures also assess damage to property and social exclusion.

Source: Adapted from Solotaroff and Pande (2014), Arango et al. (2014) and Kerr-Wilson et al. (2020).

Consequences of VAWG

Violence against women and girls has numerous detrimental short- and long-term consequences on women's and girls' physical, mental, and reproductive health. Such violence often negatively affects their children's health and wellbeing, leaving long-lasting psychological scars. VAWG incurs high psychological, social and economic costs for women, their families and societies as a whole.

VAWG can have fatal outcomes, such as homicide and suicide. IPV leads to direct injuries in 42% of affected women (WHO, 2013). Sexual violence and abuse can lead to unintended pregnancies, induced abortions, reproductive problems, and the transmission of STDs, including HIV. For example, sexually abused women are twice as likely to have an abortion (WHO, 2013). Furthermore, women who experience IPV are 16% more likely to suffer a miscarriage and 41% more likely to have a premature birth (WHO, 2013).

Women who experience intimate partner violence and abuse are more likely to report poor physical health, have adverse reproductive health outcomes, and have higher rates of alcohol abuse (WHO, 2013; Ellsberg et al., 2013; Hindin et al., 2008). Victims of VAWG are also more likely to experience depression, post-traumatic stress disorder, sleep difficulties, eating disorders, and attempt suicide (Ellsberg et al., 2008; WHO, 2013). In areas with higher HIV prevalence rates, women who experience IPV are more susceptible to HIV infections (Durevall et al., 2015; UNAIDS, 2014). Sexual violence, especially the one experienced during childhood or adolescence, can lead to substance abuse, drinking problems, and risky sexual behaviours. It is also associated with a higher likelihood of being a victim of violence later in life.

As mentioned, VAWG also affects the children of the victims. Children who grow up in families with intimate-partner violence can show various behavioural and emotional difficulties associated with their experience of witnessing VAWG. These experiences can also have long-term consequences on their physical and mental health and their likelihood of perpetrating or experiencing violence later in life.

The broader social and economic costs of VAWG are enormous and have indirect effects throughout society. For example, women can be isolated and withdrawn from closer social circles; they are less likely to participate in regular activities and have reduced capacity to care for themselves and their children. Victims of VAWG are also less likely to work and, in general, to take advantage of economic opportunities (International Rescue Committee [IRC], 2012). Indeed, some authors estimate that the financial costs of only IPV might be 5.2% of global GDP (Fearon and Hoeffler (2014).

Ecologic model of VAWG

Most recent conceptualisations of violence against women and girls have shifted from an initial focus on individual-level explanations to increasing recognition of the complex interplay of multiple environmental and individual factors (Michau et al., 2015). In this line, the WHO (2010) defined violence against women and girls as a social problem rooted in unequal power and resource distributions between men and women and institutionalised through laws, policies, and norms that ensure preferential rights to men.

The most prominent conceptualisation of the VAWG is the so-called "ecological framework" based on Bronfenbrenner's Ecological Systems Theory (Bronfenbrenner, 2009). Bronfenbrenner argues that we need to consider the entire ecological system humans grow in to understand their development. He conceptualised five sub-systems, from an individual's relationship with its immediate environment (microsystem) to institutional patterns prevalent in society (macrosystem). Heise (1998) adapted the model to the discussion of violence against women and girls, with a framework that recognises that there is no single factor that "causes" partner violence. In this framework, the VAWG results from the interaction of factors at different levels of the social environment (**Figure 4**). It starts from people's inner-most level of biological and personal history brought into their relationships. The second level is the immediate context of the interrelationship in which violence or abuse occurs (usually in the family context). The third level represents the institutions and formal and informal social structures that embed the relationships, such as neighbourhoods, workplaces, peer groups, and social networks. The fourth outermost level is the broad social and economic environment, including social norms, religion, cultural patterns and histories that shape and influence all parts of societies. And the fifth level?

The ecological framework combines personal risk factors with family, community, and society level factors identified through empirical studies. It also helps explain why some societies or individuals are more violent than others. The premise is that the likelihood that a partner will become abusive or that a community will have high rates of IPV depends on many interacting factors. The levels of interaction range from the individual and their own life experience to a couple's interaction, the household, community(s) they belong to, the wider institutional network and their society. The model's key is that all ecological levels interact to perpetuate VAWG, and positive intervention on one level can be undone or neutralised by a risk factor on another level. Hence the importance of an ecosystem view of IPV prevention.

The "ecological framework" helps gain a better understanding of the process of violence genesis, its root causes, determinants, risk factors and outcomes. Moreover, it allows for simultaneous consideration of various determinants and correlations of VAWG at different levels and forms.

Figure 4: Ecologic model of violence against women and girls (VAWG)

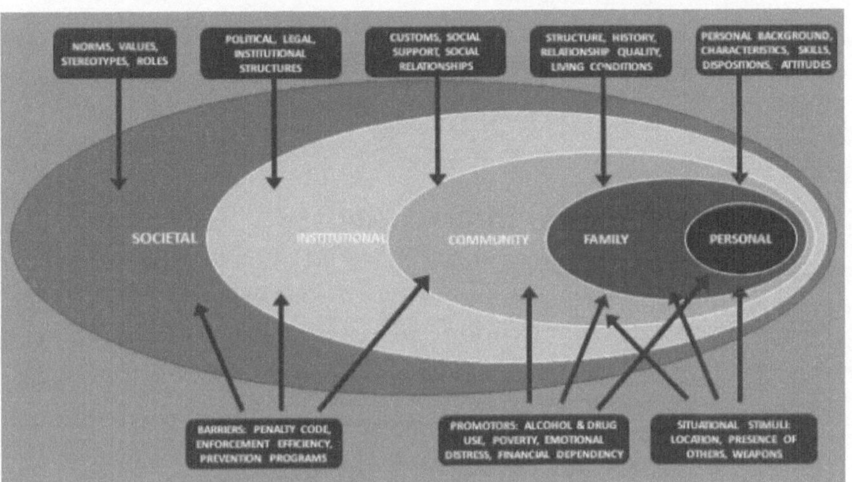
NORMS, VALUES, STEREOTYPES, ROLES
POLITICAL, LEGAL, INSTITUTIONAL STRUCTURES
CUSTOMS, SOCIAL SUPPORT, SOCIAL RELATIONSHIPS
STRUCTURE, HISTORY, RELATIONSHIP QUALITY, LIVING CONDITIONS
PERSONAL BACKGROUND, CHARACTERISTICS, SKILLS, DISPOSITIONS, ATTITUDES
SOCIETAL
INSTITUTIONAL
COMMUNITY
FAMILY
PERSONAL
BARRIERS: PENALTY CODE, ENFORCEMENT EFFICIENCY, PREVENTION PROGRAMS
PROMOTORS: ALCOHOL & DRUG USE, POVERTY, EMOTIONAL DISTRESS, FINANCIAL DEPENDENCY
SITUATIONAL STIMULI: LOCATION, PRESENCE OF OTHERS, WEAPONS

2. VAWG intervention programs

Prevalence of VAWG interventions

During the first two decades of the 21st century, VAWG has drawn the increasing attention of policymakers, activists, and researchers worldwide. Donors have also stepped up their efforts in this area in several ways. They reassessed their funding portfolios and increased funding of global initiatives to build the evidence base and identify successful interventions. For example, USAID evaluated the implementation of its global VAWG strategy in 2015. UK's Department for International Development (DfID) published an independent review of its work on VAWG. It has recently funded the £25 million, five-year *What works to prevent violence against women and girls programme*[1]. The Inter-American Development Bank has financed pilots and scaled-up initiatives, such as *Ciudad Mujer*, True Love, and the adaptation of the IMAGE programme in Peru.

As a result, a growing number of intervention programs to address VAWG have been developed and implemented. The systematic review of IPV interventions by Picon and colleagues (2017) illustrates the proliferation of these programmes and their accelerating growth over the two recent decades (**Figure 5**). Furthermore, it shows that most of the reviewed empirical evidence comes from very recent studies.

Figure 5: Number of VAWG interventions in law to middle-income countries between 2006 - 2016

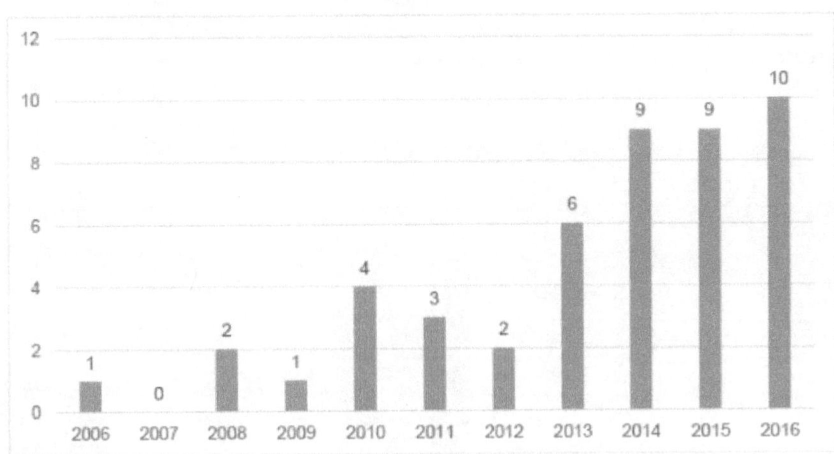

Source: Picon et al. (2017).

Forms of Violence Studied

Figure 6 presents the distribution of reviews according to VAWG types addressed in the World Bank's 2014 report (Arango et al., 2014). A majority of the reviews (59%) examined interventions aimed at reducing IPV. Around a quarter of the studies analysed evidence related to the reduction of non-partner sexual abuse. The additional 9% (five reviews) focused on findings related to several types of violence women and girls face. Two reviews related to harmful traditional practices (HTP), and only one of the selected 58 reviews solely examined female genital mutilation/cutting (FGM/C), child marriage (CM), trafficking and child sexual abuse.

Figure 6: Type of violence reviewed

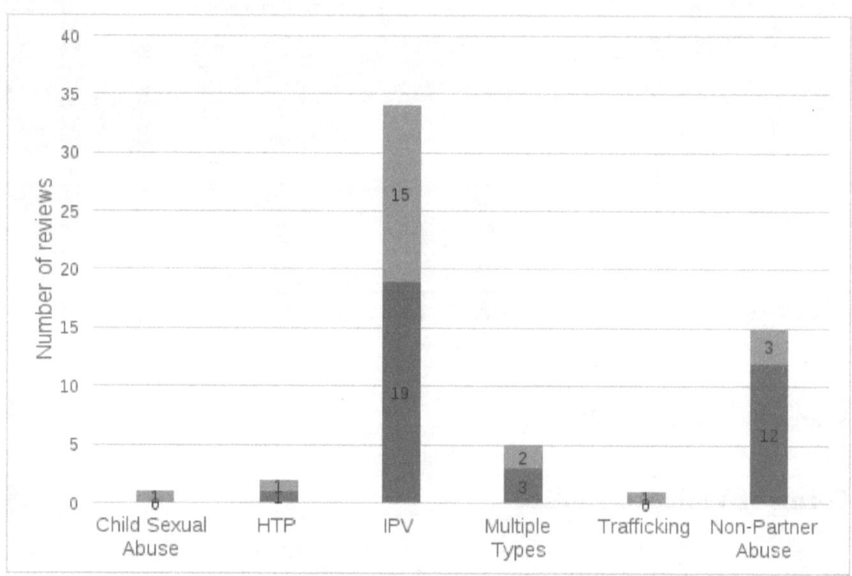

Source: Arango, Diana & Morton, Matthew & Gennari, Floriza & Kiplesund, Sveinung & Ellsberg, Mary (2014). Interventions to prevent or reduce violence against women and girls: A systematic review of reviews. http://dx.doi.org/10.13140/RG.2.1.2545.6168

After further selection of eligible impact assessment studies within selected systematic reviews, IPV studies became even more dominant, with 69 per cent (n=58) of the 84 impact evaluations identified in the review of reviews. Non-partner sexual abuse, a category that includes rape or sexual assault perpetrated by a non-intimate partner, comprises one fifth (n=17) of included individual intervention studies. Evaluations reporting effects related to change in harmful traditional practices (including FGM/C and child marriage) account for little more than one-tenth (n=9) of all evaluations (Figure 7). Unfortunately, this report did not identify any impact evaluation study satisfying the inclusion criteria for child sexual abuse or trafficking (Arango et al., 2014).

Location of the VAWG interventions

The vast majority (77%) of the selected impact evaluations were conducted in the high-income countries in North America, Western Europe, and the Pacific region. More precisely, more than three-quarters of the selected studies come from seven developed countries: Australia, Canada, Denmark, Hong Kong, New Zealand, United Kingdom, and the United States), which comprise only six per cent of the world's population (Arango et al., 2014; Ellsberg et al., 2014). Furthermore, the skewed geographical distribution of obtained empirical evidence is evident even within this group, with two-thirds of all selected studies coming from the United States and the remaining 11% from the other six high-income countries (**Figure** 7).

Figure 7: Identified VAWG interventions around the world

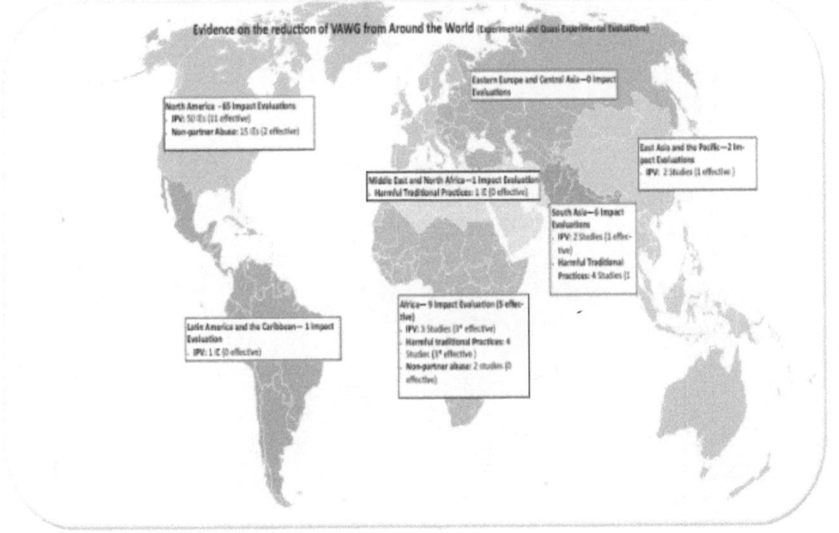

Source: Arango, Diana & Morton, Matthew & Gennari, Floriza & Kiplesund, Sveinung & Ellsberg, Mary (2014). Interventions to prevent or reduce violence against women and girls: A systematic review of reviews. http://dx.doi.org/10.13140/RG.2.1.2545.6168

However, although most of the selected studies were conducted in high-income countries, this pattern is not consistent across individual VAWG categories. For example, most studies focused on harmful traditional practices refer to LMIC countries (**Figure 8**), which probably reflects the fact that such practices are much more common across these countries. Likewise, most primary prevention programmes are implemented in LMICs, while VAWG interventions in high-income countries often focus on secondary prevention (Ellsberg et al., 2014).

Figure 8: Number of selected studies by countries income level

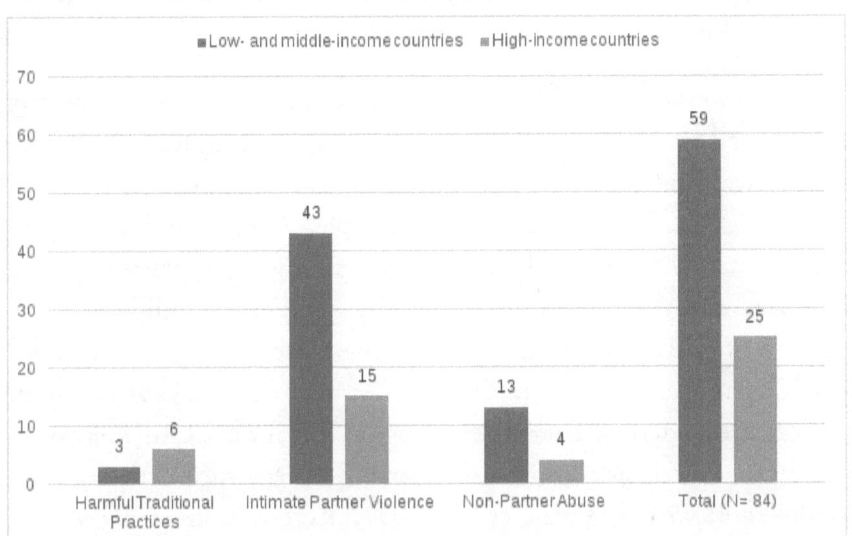

Source: Adjusted from Arango, Diana & Morton, Matthew & Gennari, Floriza & Kiplesund, Sveinung & Ellsberg, Mary (2014). Interventions to prevent or reduce violence against women and girls: A systematic review of reviews. http://dx.doi.org/10.13140/RG.2.1.2545.6168

Types of VAWG interventions

A wide variety of intervention strategies has been used in VAWG interventions, focusing on primary prevention (before violence occurs) or secondary intervention (after violence occurs). The interventions include 1) one-on-one individual therapy or training sessions, 2) work with couples and families, 3) group-based interventions (e.g. in school classes, group training, etc.), 4) community mobilisation efforts, 5) "gender transformative" programmes that aim to change system-wide social norms, gender roles and stereotypes, embedded power structures and institutional and economic inequalities. As we will see in the following sections, most VAWG interventions focus on primary or secondary prevention of IPV. Many are also aiming to reduce the incidence of non-partner abuse, child sexual abuse, harmful traditional practices, human trafficking, peer violence, etc.

VAWG interventions differ in various ways and are consequently categorized according to different criteria. There are indeed differences in the way interventions are organised and presented in multiple systematic literature reviews. For example, Arango and colleagues (2014) mainly focus on the differences among the types of violence that the interventions address. On the other hand, Ellsberg et al. (2014) evaluate intervention effectiveness separately for HIC and LMIC contexts. However, the most informative categorisation of interventions derives from the ecological framework and follows its conceptual levels. Most meta-analyses implement such categorisation (Fulu et al., 2015; Picon et al., 2017; Kerr-Wilson et al., 2020). Nevertheless, even these classifications are not always straightforward, given that some types of interventions cover more than one level of the model. Consequently, there are cases in which one group of authors placed one particular intervention in different categories.[1]

Some of the most common intervention strategies described in the available literature, which use the classification approach based on the ecological framework, are outlined in **Table 2.**

Table 2: Individual level: Studies that focus on interventions targeted at men or women, irrespective of their belonging to a community, interest group or other collectives

A1	**Economic, income generation**	Impact evaluations and systematic reviews of economic interventions and their effects on IPV prevention outcomes. The intervention itself is typically not designed to prevent IPV, but the study does look into its impact on IPV prevention and risk factors. Examples include microfinance, vocational or job training programmes, and cash transfers.
A2	**Social empowerment, skills building, awareness-raising**	Interventions focusing on social empowerment through non-economic means target mainly women (particularly from vulnerable groups) and sometimes also men. Interventions include gender sensitisation, transformative programming, awareness-raising about women's rights, access to services, protecting oneself from violence, and building soft skills or organisational skills. These interventions can be delivered to groups or one-to-one through home visits for vulnerable individuals. They may focus on health issues, family roles, violence and services available.
A3	**Attention to physical or psychological health**	Interventions that assist victims by providing physical and psychological health services and working with victimisers when psychological assistance is needed. They are considered if and only if they have a prevention component or the study deals with their effect on IPV/VAWG prevention outcomes. Physical health includes the treatment of alcohol abuse, but alcohol abuse can also be targeted through other types of interventions.
A4	**Bystander interventions**	Interventions that organise or promote action taken by a person (or persons) not directly involved as the subject or perpetrator of VAWG to identify, speak out about or seek to engage others in responding to violence. While some forms of bystander action intend to intervene in actual violent incidents, others are designed to challenge

the social norms and attitudes that perpetuate violence in the community. They can target men, boys, women or girls.

Relationship and household level: Studies of interventions targeted at i) a couple; ii) members of a couple individually if focused on their interaction; iii) other members of the household identified as key in the prevention of IPV, such as children, in-laws, parents

B1	**Counselling, critical awareness of gender roles**	These interventions include workshops and direct counselling for men and women separately or together. They encourage critical awareness of gender roles and norms, promote the position of women, challenge the distribution of resources and allocation of duties between men and women, and address the power relationships between women and others in the community.
B2	**Parenting interventions**	Interventions targeting parents who have abused or neglected their children, are at risk of doing so or utilise parental roles as a channel for gender role sensitisation. Activities include counselling, role play, media modelling of positive behaviours, structured play, production and delivery of communication materials, etc. They can be delivered through home visits, organized as community-based activities, and implemented in a health clinic or other settings.
B3	**Curriculum-based activities at school**	Interventions are delivered at school through formal courses, in-class workshops, or modification at an institutional level of the curricula or educational approaches with an IPV prevention aim.
B4	**Extra-curricular activities for children,**	Activities outside school, focused on children (under 13) or adolescents (13–17). They include sports, music, theatre and other extra-curricular activities when not

adolescents	part of a community-wide programme.	

Community-level: Interventions targeting entire communities or specific interest groups, fostering collective action through education and capacity building to address inequitable norms and practices

C1	**Communication and advocacy campaigns**	Advocacy campaigns aim to raise awareness or increase knowledge about available services, applicable laws or IPV as an issue in general. They often take the form of a regional or national coalition of individuals and organisations that are encouraged to take action to influence policy change. They often include media interventions, using television, radio, newspapers, magazines and other printed publications. In addition, campaigns include social norms marketing used to change perceptions about attitudes and behaviour considered normal by the community, to activate positive social norms and discourage harmful ones.
C2	**Community-wide mobilisation**	Community mobilisation interventions attempt to empower women, engage with men and change gender stereotypes and norms at a community level. They can take the form of community workshops and peer training to shift attitudes and behaviour by interrogating prevalent models. They are often complemented with localised campaigns and community mobilisation activities, including video, radio broadcasts or dramas.
C3	**Activities and mobilisation through common-interest groups or associations**	Activities for groups formed around shared characteristics or affiliations (churches, universities, savings groups, women's groups). For example, IPV training for microfinance groups.
C4	**Workplace and**	Sensitisation campaigns, targeted training at the

	private sector interventions	workplace, and workplace regulations.

Institutions and society level (macro-social level within the ecological framework): Interventions intended to reduce gender inequality and impact the cultural and economic factors contributing to the perpetuation of IPV by changing laws and policies and enforcing constructive existing regulations.

D1	**Awareness and advocacy focused on authorities**	Training, campaign or sensitisation programme aimed at leaders and politicians to generate change from above.
D2	**Promotion of local norms, legislation and debates**	Initiatives to establish new norms, rules or laws by fostering and enabling an environment conducive to changes in gender relations. Examples are a system of quotas for women's participation in local governance or discussion of women's issues linked to IPV during elections to encourage voting and influence the debate. Campaigns for women's equality in leadership positions belong to this category.
D3	**Police activities/ enforcement of existing laws and regulations**	Interventions focused on police or other agents responsible for enforcing existing regulations, including the judiciary system. Also, interventions that enforce health policy or legislation relevant to IPV prevention.

Emerging trends in IPV prevention: A separate grouping is considered for interventions defined not by a specific level of the ecological model but by the channel used to deliver the intervention or when the design tackles multiple levels.

E1	**ICT-based interventions**	These interventions include mobile phones, the Internet, and hotlines. While the use of mobile phones or the Internet could be part of a broader effort at one or more levels, studies try to identify evidence around its use to

		understand its impact.
E2	**Using traditions, festivals to channel messages**	Interventions in contexts in which the key mechanisms to pass information and create awareness about IPV are local traditions, ceremonies or festivals. For example, a recent impact evaluation of IPV prevention through a coffee ceremony in Ethiopia (ongoing).
E3	**Multicomponent interventions**	Studies evaluating interventions that operate across different levels of the social ecology, either considering the programme as a whole or multiple interventions at more than one level of the social ecology. For example, an intervention looking to empower women by training them in soft skills while also providing relationship counselling belongs to this category. Also, a study that reports on the overall effect of a programme looking to influence multiple levels, such as SASA! project.[2]

Source: Picon et al. (2017).

Prevalence of different types of VAWG interventions

The above-presented classification of VAWG interventions is outlined in the World Bank's meta-analysis.[3] Here we show which type of interventions were covered in selected 84 impact assessment studies, considering whether they were primary or secondary preventions (**Figure 9**). Some interventions are characteristic of specific VAWG categories. For example, batterer interventions (reducing recidivism among perpetrators of violence) are the most common in the IPV category. Group training in primary prevention was the most frequent approach in the NPA category. Livelihood interventions and community mobilisation in primary prevention were the most frequent intervention methods in the HTP category.

Figure 9: Number of selected studies by type of intervention

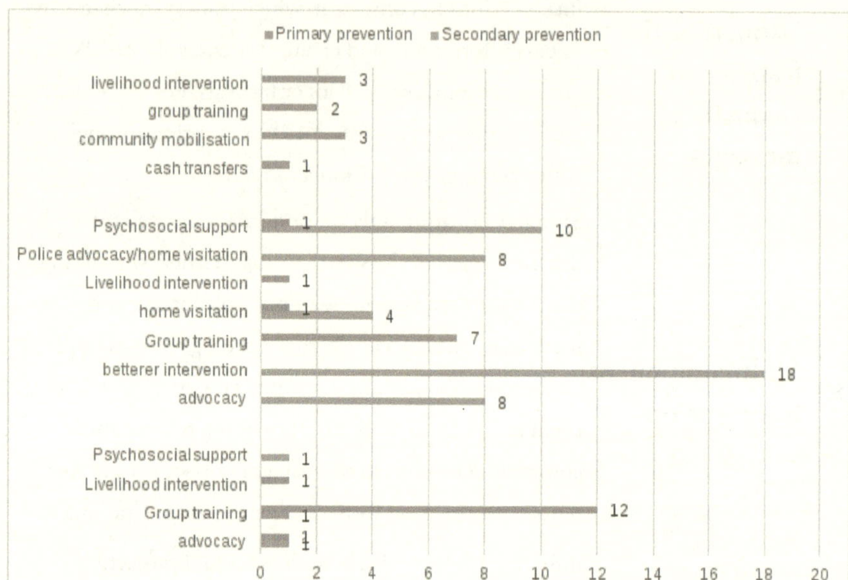

Source: Adjusted from Arango et al. (2014). Interventions to prevent or reduce violence against women and girls: A systematic review of reviews. http://dx.doi.org/10.13140/RG.2.1.2545.6168

Characteristics of the VAWG interventions

Intervention programs in the area of VAWG come in all shapes and forms in terms of their size, duration, scope, target group, sample sizes, impact assessment design (in cases where there are any), etc. In the following paragraphs, we will shortly outline some of the main characteristics of those VAWG intervention programmes that have implemented the impact assessment process.

Impact Evaluation (IE) Design

More than two-thirds of the selected VAWG studies (70%) were randomized   control   trials   (RCTs),   with   quasi-experiments representing the remaining 30% of the included reviews (**Figure 10**). Quasi-experiments were more dominant in the Harmful Traditional Practices (HTP) category.

Figure 10: Number of selected studies by impact evaluation design

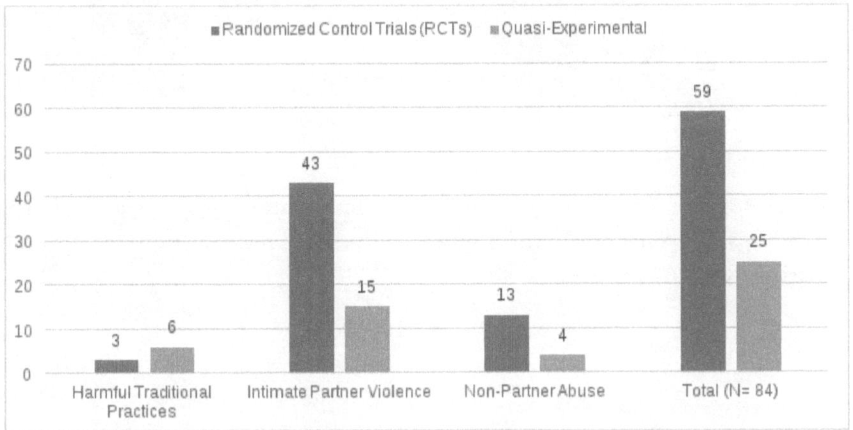

Source: Adjusted from Arango et al. (2014). Interventions to prevent or reduce violence against women and girls: A systematic review of reviews. http://dx.doi.org/10.13140/RG.2.1.2545.6168

Sample size

Sample sizes in most of the selected studies consisted of 300 or more participants (**Figure 11**). However, in the Non-Partner Abuse (NPA) studies, sample sizes were often smaller, while in the HTP category, no data was provided on the sample sizes.

Figure 11: Number of selected studies by sample size

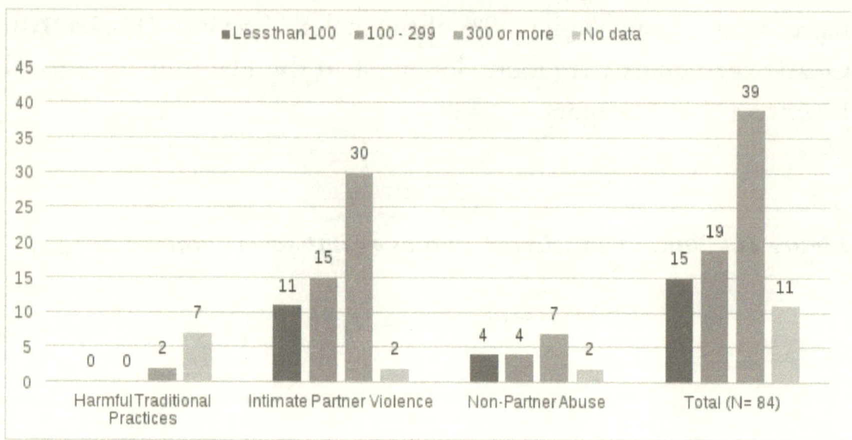

Source: Adjusted from Arango et al. (2014). Interventions to prevent or reduce violence against women and girls: A systematic review of reviews. http://dx.doi.org/10.13140/RG.2.1.2545.6168

Participants' age

The great majority of the IPV studies work either with adults or all age groups (**Figure 12**). On the other hand, studies from the HTP and NPA categories focus much more on adolescents and youth. Surprisingly, only 5% of selected studies included children and early adolescence.

Figure 12: Number of selected studies by participants' age

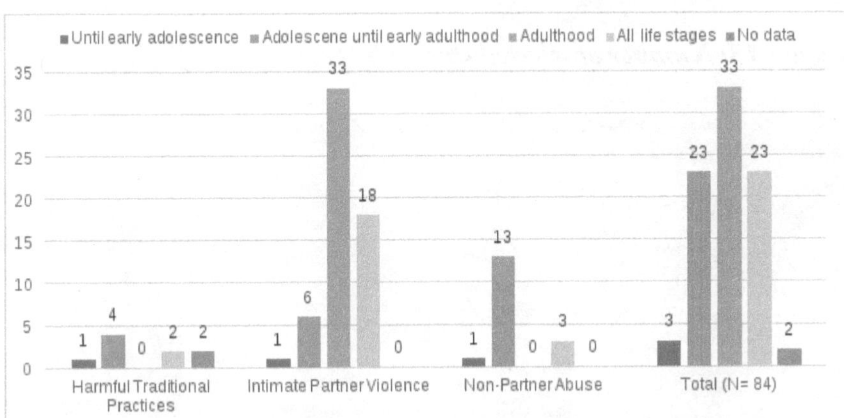

Source: Adjusted from Arango et al. (2014). Interventions to prevent or reduce violence against women and girls: A systematic review of reviews. http://dx.doi.org/10.13140/RG.2.1.2545.6168

Participants' gender

More than half of the evaluated studies (51%) are focused solely on women and girls, with the remaining half working either with only men (29%) or with both women and men (20%). Studies addressing HTP are exceptions from this pattern, with most of them working either with both genders or with only women and girls (**Figure 13**).

Figure 13: Number of selected studies by participants' gender

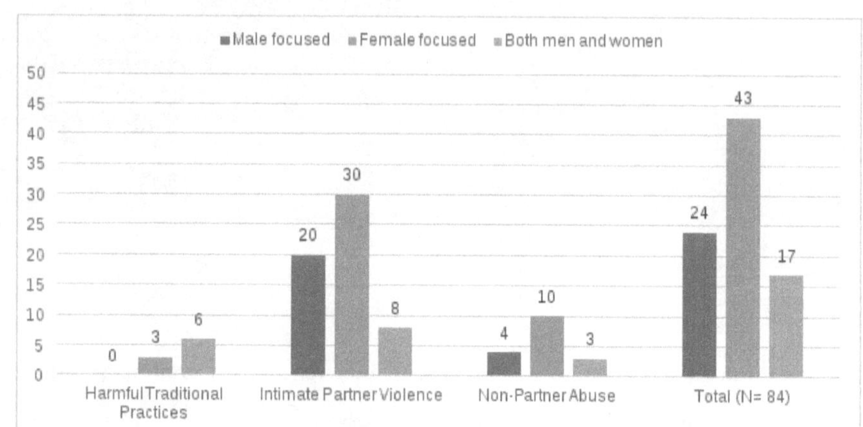

Source: Adjusted from Arango et al. (2014). Interventions to prevent or reduce violence against women and girls: A systematic review of reviews. http://dx.doi.org/ 10.13140/RG.2.1.2545.6168

Moment of intervention (before or after violence occurs)

There are two types of interventions in this area regarding the moment when they are applied: primary preventions and secondary interventions. Primary prevention refers to reducing the number of new instances of violence by intervening before violence takes place. Secondary intervention refers to mitigating the immediate consequences of abuse by providing already-abused women and girls with services and support and, more pertinently in the field of VAWG interventions, preventing the recurrence of abuse.

There were more secondary interventions among the selected impact assessment studies, although this proportion greatly varied across different categories of VAWG (**Figure 14**). For example, the IPV studies overwhelmingly focus on secondary interventions, while studies in HTP and NPA mainly include primary preventions.

Figure 14: Number of selected studies by the moment of intervention

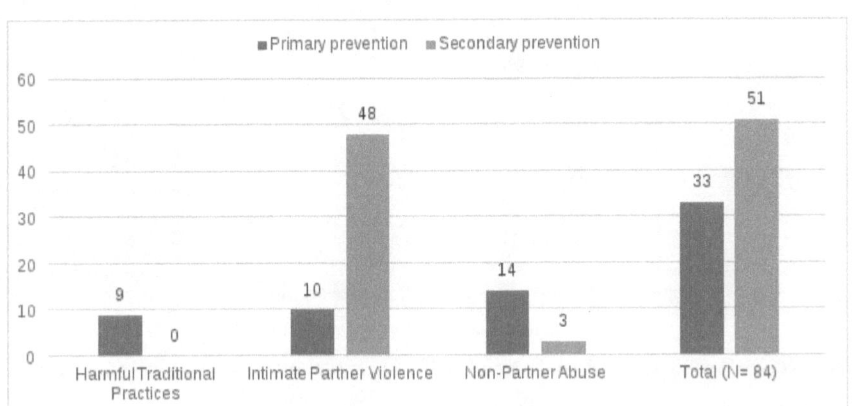

Source: Adjusted from Arango et al. (2014). Interventions to prevent or reduce violence against women and girls: A systematic review of reviews. http://dx.doi.org/ 10.13140/RG.2.1.2545.6168

Duration of intervention

Most interventions lasted a few months, with a relatively high average frequency or dosage of the interventions, at least 10 hours long, occurring over several weeks or months (Arango et al., 2014) (**Figure 15**). The most extended intervention was a home visitation program that took place over three years (Duggan et al., 1999). However, most of the interventions in the area of Non-Partner Abuse took the form of a single event, thus raising doubts about their effectiveness and the potential duration of any positive effects.

Figure 15: Number of selected studies by the duration of intervention

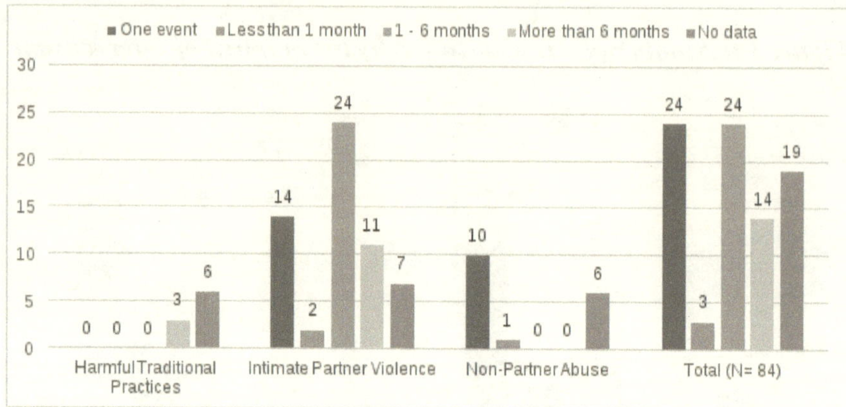

Source: Adjusted from Arango et al. (2014). Interventions to prevent or reduce violence against women and girls: A systematic review of reviews. http://dx.doi.org/10.13140/RG.2.1.2545.6168

3. Effectiveness of VAWG intervention programs

Systematic reviews of intervention programs

With the increasing number of VAWG interventions and the accumulation of empirical evidence of their effectiveness, there was a growing need for systematic overview reviews and meta-analyses of such evidence. Indeed, in recent years groups of international experts have published several significant reports, reviewing evidence from all across the world and assessing various types of interventions, programmes and policies.

The most important, rigorous and systematic among these are the two overlapping reviews. The first is a policy report commissioned by the World Bank (WB) and conducted by Arango and colleagues (2014). The second is an academic article written by Ellsberg and colleagues (2014) and published in the leading scientific journal Lancet. These are the first systematic reviews of reviews that synthesize evidence on the effects of VAWG prevention interventions. Before the WB report, evidence of program effectiveness was analysed and presented less systematically and comprehensively in other studies, such as the In-depth Study on all forms of violence against women: a report to the Secretary-General of the UN in 2006 and the Population Reports: Ending Violence Against Women written by Lori Heise, Mary Ellsberg and Megan Gottemoeller in 1999.

The 2014 meta-analysis by the World Bank represents a systematic review of reviews synthesizing evidence from all reviews assessing the reported effects of prevention interventions to reduce violence against women. This meta-analysis is of excellent quality because it was conducted according to the guidelines provided in the Cochrane Handbook for Systematic Reviews of Interventions (Green & Higgins, 2009) and consistently adhered to the established scientific practices in selecting and reviewing empirical evidence. Impact evaluations from individual reviews were eligible for inclusion in this meta-analysis if they contained experimental or quasi-experimental designs with well-defined comparison groups[4]. The WB meta-review included two groups of individual reviews in its analysis:

- **Systematic reviews**: as defined by the Cochrane Handbook (Green & Higgins, 2009), a systematic review attempts to identify, appraise, and synthesize all the empirical evidence that meets pre-specified eligibility criteria to answer a given research question.

- **Comprehensive reviews**: reviews that did not meet the abovementioned systematic review criteria but have tried to review and describe the evidence on the impacts of interventions to reduce VAWG. To be selected, their primary objective was to examine the evidence of the effects of interventions designed to prevent or reduce VAWG. They also needed to review results from at least two impact evaluations.

The review in total examined evidence from 290 tested interventions. Topics covered include child sexual abuse, sexual harassment, female genital mutilation/cutting, forced/child marriage and other harmful traditional practices, psychological/emotional abuse, physical assault, trafficking, and similar damaging activities.

Apart from the World Bank report, Ellsberg and colleagues (2014) published another excellent meta-analysis on the same topic in the same year. The two meta-reviews are very similar in their methods, reviewed studies and findings. Therefore, we will use their results interchangeably in the remainder of this report.

Fulu and colleagues (2015) have published a rapid review of available empirical evidence on VAWG programme's effectiveness in the following year. The review was composed as a baseline overview of the needs of the DFID's then newly-established programme *"What Works to Prevent Violence Against Women and Girls"*. However, the authors did not implement a systematic review and did not use standard criteria to evaluate programme effectiveness.

Two years later, Picon and colleagues (2017) from *The International Initiative for Impact Evaluation (3ie)* published another systematic review of available empirical evidence in this area. Although bringing further insight into this field, especially regarding the characteristics and prevalence of VAWG interventions in LMIcs, this review was not as comprehensive as the World Bank's or the two conducted within the DFID's "What Works" programme (the second published in 2020). First of all, this review focused only on interventions undertaken in the LMIC context. It also reviews only interventions aiming at the primary prevention of IPV. Finally, and most importantly, this systematic review does not assess the effectiveness of reviewed programmes but mainly focuses on describing their characteristics and prevalence.

Experts from DFID's "What Works" programme compiled another review of the empirical evidence at the end of their five-year programme. This report, authored by Kerr-Wilson and colleagues (2020), compliments previous reviews with new research studies and empirical evidence. The authors conducted this review more thoroughly and systematically than the previous DFID review by Fulu and colleagues. However, Kerr-Wilson et al. study (2020) also did not implement some of the established scientific criteria for evaluating the effectiveness of reviewed interventions. Instead, they established their own ad hoc criteria, which were somewhat loose, inconsistent and even contradictory. For example, although they had outlined four possible outcomes of their evaluation ("effective", "promising", "conflicting", "no effect"), their definition of "conflicting" outcome entirely overlaps with their definition of "effective" outcomes.[5] This situation means that all of their outcomes assessed as "effective" are simultaneously "conflicting", following their ad hoc criteria. However, both DFID reports are highly informative and offer a wealth of new information that directly complements the World Bank reports from 2014. So, in the following chapters, we will present the evidence compiled from all five reviews. But when evaluating the effectiveness of VAWG interventions, we will mainly rely on the findings provided in the two World Bank reports (Arango et al., 2014 & Ellsberg et al., 2014). In cases where specific categories of VAWG interventions were not evaluated in the World Bank reports but were only assessed in "What Works" reports, we will classify these evaluations into three categories: "promising", "conflicting", and "not-effective" (and exclude the problematic "effective" category).

The main characteristics of the five systematic reviews serving as a basis of our report are outlined in **Table 3**.

Table 3: Characteristics of the systematic reviews of empirical evidence in the area of VAWG

	Arango et al. (2014)	Ellsberg et al. (2014)	Fulu et al. (2015)	Picon et al. (2017)	Kerr-Wilson et al. (2020)
Type of review	Systematic review of reviews	Systematic review of reviews	Rapid review (non-systematic)	Systematic review of reviews	Systematic review of reviews
Scope	Global	Global	Global	LMICs	Global with emphasis on LMICs
Type of violence	VAWG: IPV, HTP, NPA	VAWG: IPV, HTP, NPA	VAWG: IPV, NPA, CSA, CAM	Primary IPV interventions	VAWG: IPV, NPA, CPV
Criteria for inclusion	RCT; quasi-experiments	RCT; quasi-experiments	Any type of impact evaluation	RCT; quasi-exp; PSM; RDD; SR	RCT; quasi-exp.; 'What Works' studies
Number of reviews	58	58	24	0	12
Number of individual interventions	84	84	244	47 (+28 ongoing)	104
Quality evaluation criteria	Strict (Cochrane study)	Strict (Cochrane study)	Loose ad hoc criteria	Not used	Loose ad hoc criteria
Time period of evaluation	2000 - 2013	2000 - 2013	2000 - 2014	2000 - 2016	2000 - 2019
Funded by	World Bank	World Bank & Australian government	DFID (What Works to Prevent Violence)	International Initiative for Impact Evaluation (3ie)	DFID (What Works to Prevent Violence)
Published as	Policy report	Academic paper	Policy report	Policy report	Policy report

Note: SR-Systematic Reviews; PSM - Propensity Score Matching: RDD - Regression Discontinuity Design; IPV - Intimate partner violence; NPA - non-partner abuse; CSA - child sexual abuse; CAM - child abuse & maltreatment; CPV - child peer violence.

Main findings from reviews

Overall findings

Of all the 84 interventions using an experimental or quasi-experimental study design and summarized in included World Bank reviews, the overwhelming majority (70%) had no recorded impact on the targeted VAWG outcomes (Arango et al., 2014; Ellsberg et al., 2014). Around one in ten reviewed studies had an evident significant positive effect. An additional 14% of studies had a positive but 'mixed' effect, indicating that obtained findings were positive on some, but not all, measured outcomes. Finally, in around 5% of assessed interventions, the impact was assessed as significantly negative or identified significant adverse outcomes (**Figure 16**).

Figure 16: Impact assessment across selected studies by type of violence

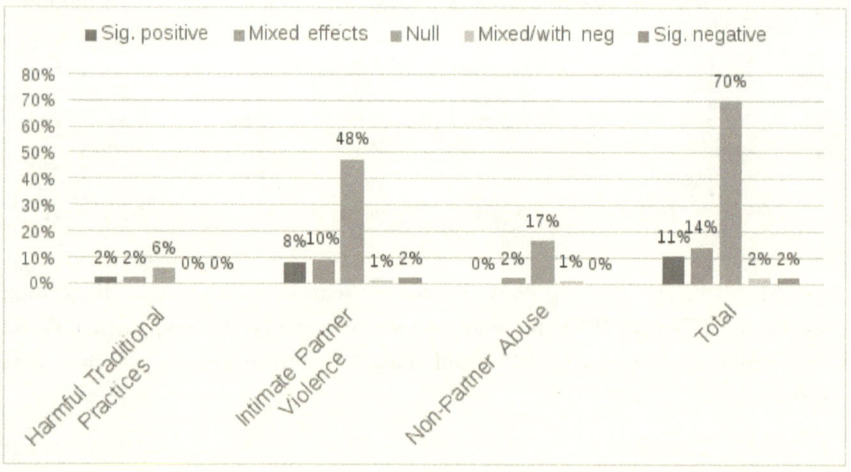

Source: Adjusted from Arango et al. (2014). Interventions to prevent or reduce violence against women and girls: A systematic review of reviews. http://dx.doi.org/10.13140/RG.2.1.2545.6168

Findings by the type of intervention

The two meta-analytic studies of the effectiveness of VAWG interventions (Arango et al., 2014; Ellsberg et al., 2014) provide a valuable overview of the findings of VAWG program effectiveness across different categories of violence and country income levels. We will present the key findings from these overviews in the following paragraphs.

Table 4: Individual-level intervention programmes

Intervention strategy: Individual-level change	Example	Type of violence	Economic context	
			High-income countries	Low- and middle-income countries
Social empowerment of vulnerable groups	Interventions with female sex workers, pregnant women, women with mental disabilities, vulnerable drug users, and marginalised girls.	IPV, NPSA	*Not applicable*	*Promising*
Education of men and boys to prevent VAWG	Participatory group education around concepts of masculinity and inequitable gender attitudes and behaviours		*Insufficient evidence*	*Promising*
Bystander interventions primarily targeting men and boys	Interventions that encourage men and boys not directly involved as subjects or perpetrators of violence to speak out or engage others in response to violence. Based on the recognition that men can be allies in preventing sexual assault	IPV, NPSA	*Conflicting*	*Not applicable*
Tackling alcohol abuse	1) screening in primary care settings, early detection; 2) restricted access to alcohol (laws, policies, prices); 3) community-based interventions, changing the drinking environment; 4) treatment and self-help support systems, such as AA	IPV, HIV-risk	*Promising*	*Insufficient evidence*
Self-defence training to prevent sexual assault	Alongside physical self-defence strategies, training includes lectures and group activities on positive sexuality, rape myths, risk factors and risk assessment, emotional barriers to resistance, etc.	NPSA, IPV	*Promising (college)/ Conflicting (schools)*	*Promising (college)/ Conflicting (schools)*
Interventions in antenatal and postnatal settings	Almost exclusively in HIC. 1) Psycho-behavioural counselling, safety planning, legal and financial advice, and 2) nurse-visitation programmes during and after pregnancy	IPV	*Conflicting*	*Not applicable*
Interventions to reduce alcohol and drug use	CBT-based couples' interventions; community-based interventions; treatment and self-help support systems; structural interventions	IPV, NPSA	*Effective in reducing alcohol use*	*Effective in reducing alcohol use*

Social empowerment of vulnerable groups (Fulu et al., 2015): Mostly addressed vulnerable groups are female sex workers (FSW), pregnant women, women with disabilities, health problems or HIV, etc. Interventions based on social empowerment involve group work with women and girls from a similar background or one-on-one support for particularly vulnerable individuals (through home visits by health workers). Interventions combine awareness-raising (about their rights, available services, self-protection means) with skill-building (collective organising, leadership, self-defence, alternative livelihood, etc.).

<u>Effectiveness of interventions</u>: Avahan HIV prevention programme in Karnataka (Blanchard, 2013; Karnataka Health Promotion Trust, 2012) and especially Ashodaya Samithi initiative in Mysore (Reza-Paul et al., 2012), both with sex workers, showed a significant decrease in violence perpetrated by clients and police.

Education of men and boys to prevent VAWG (Kerr-Wilson, 2020): programmes aiming to engage men as allies of women in VAWG prevention. An example with a positive impact is the Yaari Dosti intervention (India), based on "Program H" developed by the Brazilian organisation Promundo. The programme promotes positive aspects of masculinity, encourages men's sexual and reproductive health participation, and promotes respect for sexual diversity. At the end of the programme, there was a significant decrease in VAW in the intervention arms compared to the control arm (Verma et al., 2008)

Bystander interventions primarily targeting men and boys (Fulu & Kerr-Wilson, 2015): Interventions mainly implemented in US schools. They can be brief one-off or longer, sometimes integrated into holistic community-based interventions. Teachers, coaches and trained educators are key figures in changing awareness and attitudes towards gender roles, violence and rape myth acceptance.

<u>Effectiveness of interventions</u>: Out of 13 assessed interventions (in Fulu et al., 2015), only one found positive outcomes (Coaching Boys into Men, Miller et al., 2012) in terms of reduced bystander support of negative behaviour of peers and, consequently, less abuse perpetration.

Tackling alcohol abuse (Fulu & Kerr-Wilson, 2015): Interventions applied on various levels, including structural restrictions through law and policies, community-based education and public dialogue, as well as treatments, therapies and self-help groups.

<u>Effectiveness of interventions</u>: There is fair evidence from HICs that structural alcohol reduction interventions positively impact reducing IPV (e.g. a longitudinal study conducted in Australia, Livingston et al., 2008). However, many detoxification treatments and couple therapies that proved successful in HIC are not affordable in LMIC. On the other hand, the low-cost model of self-help groups (e.g. implemented through religious organisations in Latin America) does not allow evaluation through RCT as it contradicts their philosophy of being open to everybody. Nevertheless, propensity score matching showed significant effects of this model of interventions.

Response to violence against women

A set of VAWG interventions is based on the secondary prevention responses implemented in situations where violence has already occurred. (**Table 5**) Among the various strategies within this category, the only approach that has garnered promising results is "victim advocacy". This approach consists of support in the case management, connecting the victim to legal services, providing necessary information, and other victim advocacy services. In the high-income context, women-centred programs for survivors and perpetrator programs have conflicting evidence. Other approaches in this category (shelters, one-stop crisis centres and women's policy stations) either do not have applicable data or have insufficient evidence. In LMIC countries, there is insufficient data on the efficiency of all of the approaches in this category.

Table 5: Intervention strategy: Response to violence against women

	Example	Type of violence	Economic context	
			High-income countries	Low- and middle-income countries
Women-centred programmes for survivors	Psychosocial counselling, post-exposure prophylaxis and emergency contraception as needed, risk assessment, referrals, safety planning	IPV, NPSA	*Conflicting*	*Insufficient evidence*
Perpetrators programmes	Interventions for men who assault their female partners	IPV	*Conflicting*	*Insufficient evidence*
One-stop crisis centres	Multidisciplinary crisis centres (community or hospital-based)	IPV, NPSA	*Not applicable or no evidence*	*Insufficient evidence*
Shelters	Safe accommodations that provide short-term refuge and other services	IPV	*Insufficient evidence*	*Insufficient evidence*
Women's police stations	Specialised police services for survivors of violence against women can include psychosocial counselling and referrals	IPV, NPSA	*Not applicable or no evidence*	*Insufficient evidence*
Victim Advocacy	Case management, connection to legal services and information	IPV	*Promising*	*Insufficient evidence*
ICT services	National emergency hotlines or mobile applications	IPV, NPSA	*Insufficient evidence*	*Insufficient evidence*

Source: Adapted from: Ellsberg, Mary & Arango, Diana & Morton, Matthew & Gennari, Floriza & Kiplesund, Sveinung & Contreras, Manuel & Watts, Charlotte. (2014). Prevention of Violence against Women and Girls: What Does the Evidence Say?. The Lancet. http://dx.doi.org/10.1016/S0140-6736(14)61703-7

Note: Programmes will often incorporate multiple components and overlaps reflecting more than one intervention type. Presented results are based on trials, including randomized controlled trials (RCTs) or quasi-experimental trials with comparison groups. IPV=intimate partner violence. NPSA=non-partner sexual assault. FGM=female genital mutilation. CM=child marriage.

Group-based training or workshops for the prevention of violence against women and girls

Most primary violence prevention programmes in LMIC contexts use participatory group training, which involves a series of educational meetings or workshops with targeted groups of participants (Ellsberg, 2014) (**Table 6**). These programmes are often embedded in broader interventions that aim to improve the health and wellbeing of women and girls. Their goal is usually broader than just preventing violence, often including components to address underlying gender norms and stereotypes and promote the development of new communication and conflict resolution skills.

The programme Fourth R (Wolfe et al., 2009), for example, is a 21-lesson curriculum with skills training for dating relationships in Canada. Recent examples of school-based interventions with positive findings on dating violence (Kerr-Wilson, 2020) include a multi-component, after-school HIV-prevention intervention ('PREPARE') in South Africa (Mathews et al., 2016) and 'Green dot' bystander training in US high schools (Coker et al., 2017).

Peer violence is systematically analysed in the review of reviews conducted by Lester, Lawrence, and Ward (2017). The vast majority of studies in this review are from HICs, and only eight are from LMICs. Kerr-Wilson report (2020) focused on interventions with a gender component and good evidence that peer violence can be prevented through school-based interventions and that their results can be sustained.

The reports from 2015 (Fulu et al.) and 2020 (Kerr-Wilson et al.) recognise two additional categories of interventions: relationship-level (or couple's) interventions and parenting programmes. Brief couple's interventions focus on health behaviours and happen in a health care setting, while intensive interventions, targeting couples from the general population, implement gender equity skill-building programmes through participatory methods. There is good evidence that couples' interventions, especially when also addressing alcohol abuse, are impactful in reducing IPV (e.g. Indashyikirwa programme in Rwanda (Dunkle et al., 2019); the VATU programme in Zambia (Murray et al., 2019), etc.). General parenting programmes have good outcomes, but their impact on IPV is rarely analysed. Recent interventions, however, combine this approach with the prevention of IPV. Although still rare, parenting programmes that explicitly address IPV show good evidence of effectiveness in reducing IPV (e.g. Bandebereho in Rwanda (Doyle et al., 2018); Family Foundations in the US (Feinberg et al., 2016), etc.).

Most of these programmes are applied in the LMIC contexts, resulting in the lack of empirical evidence on their effectiveness in high-income countries. However, in the LMIC, some of these programmes have shown substantive positive effects. Among these are group-based programmes applied with either women and girls only or with women and men. Group-based training with only men and boys has unclear effectiveness. Similarly, there is insufficient evidence of the effectiveness of approaches based on the organisation of alternative "rites of passage" ceremonies in the LMIC context (in the high-income countries, they are rarely applicable due to a lack of such practices in these contexts).

Table 6: Intervention strategy: Group-based training

	Example	Type of violence	Economic context	
			High-income countries	Low- and middle-income countries
Empowerment training for women and girls	School or community programmes to improve women's agency. Can include other components such as safe spaces, mentoring, life skills, or self-defence training	IPV, NPSA, FGM, CM	*Insufficient evidence*	*Promising*
Men and boys norms programming	School programmes and community workshops and training to promote changes in social norms (especially the rigid norms related to manhood) and behaviour that encourages violence against women and girls and gender inequality	IPV, NPSA	*Insufficient evidence*	*Conflicting*
Group training with women and men	School or community workshops to promote changes in norms and behaviour that encourage violence against women and girls and gender inequality	IPV, NPSA	*Insufficient evidence*	*Promising*
Alternative rites of passage	Training for girls in life skills culminating in a ceremony without FGM	FGM	*Not applicable or no evidence*	*Insufficient evidence*
Relationship-level interventions	Workshops aimed to develop communication and conflict resolution skills, and psychological therapies for couples addressing learnt behaviour and childhood trauma	IPV	*Not applicable*	*Promising*
Parenting programmes	Interventions aimed to reduce harsh parenting and child abuse, a risk factor for VAW later in life. Home visits, counselling in health clinic settings based on educational communication, role play, guided play between parents and children	IPV, CM	*Promising*	*Promising*
School-based (institutional) interventions	The teaching of specific gender-themed curricula, teacher training, gender-responsive pedagogy, children's clubs, as well as engagement of various stakeholders at the school level (teachers, pupils, parents, reporting mechanisms, government)	IPV, CM	*Insufficient evidence*	*Insufficient evidence*

Source: Adapted from: Ellsberg, Mary & Arango, Diana & Morton, Matthew & Gennari, Floriza & Kiplesund, Sveinung & Contreras, Manuel & Watts, Charlotte. (2014). Prevention of Violence against Women and Girls: What Does the Evidence Say?. The Lancet. http://dx.doi.org/10.1016/S0140-6736(14)61703-7

Note: Programmes will often incorporate multiple components and overlaps reflecting more than one intervention type. Presented results are based on trials, including randomized controlled trials (RCTs) or quasi-experimental trials with comparison groups. IPV=intimate partner violence. NPSA=non-partner sexual assault. FGM=female genital mutilation. CM=child marriage.

Population-based prevention

Community mobilisation campaigns aim to reduce violence at the population level through changes in public discourse, practices, and norms for gender and violence (Ellsberg et al., 2014). They have "promising" results in LMIC contexts, while they were either not applicable or had no robust impact evaluations in the high-income countries. Despite their relatively high prevalence (at the global, regional or national level), awareness-raising campaigns are found to be ineffective in both low- and high-income contexts. On the other hand, there is insufficient evidence on the efficacy of social marketing campaigns or edutainment (education through entertainment activities) across all economic contexts. Kerr-Wilson and colleagues (2020) found one recent study (a five year long, US university-based social norms marketing campaign, Mennicke et al., 2018) with a positive effect on gender norms and values but insufficient evaluation evidence. So, the conclusion is that social marketing campaigns may have a role when combined with other components of interventions at a community level.

Recent good examples of effective community mobilisation projects are (Kerr-Wilson, 2020): Transforming Masculinities in DRC (Le Roux et al., 2019), Rural Response System in Ghana (Ogum-Alangea et al., 2019). These interventions needed a strong design and implementation to effectively reduce IPV and involved multi-year intensive community mobilisation.

Table 7: Intervention strategy: Population-based prevention

	Example	Type of violence	Economic context	
			High-income countries	Low- and middle-income countries
Community mobilisation	Participatory projects (workshops and peer-training), community-driven development engaging multiple stakeholders and addressing gender norms	IPV, NPSA, FGM, CM	*Not applicable or no evidence*	*Promising*
Awareness-raising campaigns	One-off information or media efforts, billboards, radio programmes, posters, television advertisements	IPV, NPSA, FGM, CM	*Ineffective*	*Ineffective*
Social marketing campaigns or edutainment plus group education	Long-term programmes engaging social media, social media, mobile applications, thematic television series, posters, together with interpersonal communication activities	IPV, NPSA, FGM, CM	*Insufficient evidence*	*Insufficient evidence*

Source: Adapted from: Ellsberg, Mary & Arango, Diana & Morton, Matthew & Gennari, Floriza & Kiplesund, Sveinung & Contreras, Manuel & Watts, Charlotte. (2014). Prevention of Violence against Women and Girls: What Does the Evidence Say?. The Lancet. http://dx.doi.org/10.1016/S0140-6736(14)61703-7

Note: Programmes will often incorporate multiple components and overlaps reflecting more than one intervention type. Presented results are based on trials, including randomized controlled trials (RCTs) or quasi-experimental trials with comparison groups. IPV=intimate partner violence. NPSA=non-partner sexual assault. FGM=female genital mutilation. CM=child marriage.

Economic empowerment and livelihoods

The relationship between intimate partner violence and poverty – at the household and the broader community level – has been long-established both in empirical research and intervention settings. That is why some approaches to VAWG prevention have focused on increasing women's economic opportunities as a key pillar. However, the evidence of the effectiveness of such strategies is scarce and mixed, especially when it comes to the sustainability of economic intervention impact.

Such approaches are often not straightforwardly applicable in high-income countries due to women's relatively good living standards and usually solid access to various financing options. On the other hand, in LMIC contexts, interventions based on increased access to microfinance and assets have been found to both improve or worsen women's risk of violence (**Table 8**). What seems to be making a difference among them is the context in which women live. Reviews found that programs that combine economic components with additional forms of interventions, such as gender equality or skill-building training, show more promising results than those that rely only on the economic approach.

Table 8: Intervention strategy: Economic and livelihoods

	Example	Type of violence	Economic context	
			High-income countries	Low- and middle-income countries
Direct transfers of cash, food or food stamps	Nationwide governmental interventions or smaller scale non-governmental interventions, sometimes combined with nutrition training sessions; conditioned transfers for school attendance, vaccination etc.	IPV, CM	*Not applicable*	*Promising*
Economic empowerment and income supplements	Microfinance; vocational training or job placement; cash or asset transfers (e.g., land reform)	IPV, NPSA, FGM, CM	*Not applicable or no evidence*	*Conflicting*
Economic empowerment and income supplements plus gender equality training	Microfinance; vocational training or job placement; cash or asset transfers (e.g., land reform) plus gender equality and violence prevention training	IPV, NPSA, FGM, CM	*Not applicable or no evidence*	*Promising*
Retraining for traditional excisors	Microfinance or vocational training	FGM	*Not applicable or no evidence*	*Ineffective*

Source: Adapted from: Ellsberg, Mary & Arango, Diana & Morton, Matthew & Gennari, Floriza & Kiplesund, Sveinung & Contreras, Manuel & Watts, Charlotte. (2014). Prevention of Violence against Women and Girls: What Does the Evidence Say?. The Lancet. http://dx.doi.org/10.1016/S0140-6736(14)61703-7

Note: Programmes will often incorporate multiple components and overlaps reflecting more than one intervention type. Presented results are based on trials, including randomized controlled trials (RCTs) or quasi-experimental trials with comparison groups. IPV=intimate partner violence. NPSA=non-partner sexual assault. FGM=female genital mutilation. CM=child marriage.

Direct transfers of cash, food or food stamps (Kerr-Wilson et al., 2020): Of 13 RCT/quasi-experimental intervention evaluations, seven were found to have positive, two promising, and four had no impact on IVF. Among the programs implemented after 2014, those that particularly stand out are a conditional cash transfer for schooling in South Africa (Pettifor et al., 2018), World Food Program in Ecuador (Hidrobo et al., 2016) and a cash transfer and nutrition discussion in Bangladesh (Roy et al., 2018). Little is known about the sustainability of positive effects of these and similar programs. There is also a lack of evidence on whether direct targeting of women achieves better outcomes than targeting the head of the household.

Economic empowerment plus gender equality training (Kerr-Wilson et al., 2020): Programmes that combine economic and social empowerment components are more successful than programmes based exclusively on financial transfers or livelihood. Besides the effective IMAGE programme in South Africa (Pronyk et al., 2006), recent good examples include long-term multi-component programmes for adolescent girls in Uganda (Bandiera et al., 2018) and Kenya (Austrian et al., 2018), which combine microfinance/cash transfers with vocational training and violence prevention discussions. On the other side, less intensive short-term interventions showed little evidence of reducing girls' experience of IPV.

System-wide approaches

Among the various system-wide approaches more broadly implemented – usually nationally – the evidence on the interventions' effectiveness is either lacking or indicates no measurable benefits (**Table 9**). The only approach in this category that has shown promising results is the programme of home visits by health workers and nurses to reduce IPV incidences. But even for this approach, evidence from the LMIC contexts is insufficient. Infrastructure improvements have not resulted in a measurable decrease in the incidence of non-partner sexual attacks in studies that have evaluated their outcomes. Screening by nurses and doctors during hospital visits was found to be ineffective in high-income countries, while no sufficient evidence exists from LMIC countries. Personal sensitisation training of various officials (police officers, teachers, health workers, etc.) had no distinguishable positive effects in impact evaluation studies in high-income countries or LMIC contexts.

Table 9: Intervention strategy: System-wide approaches

	Example	Type of violence	Economic context	
			High-income countries	LMICs
Screening	Universal IPV screening among nurses and doctors at all visits	IPV, NPSV	*Ineffective*	*Not applicable or no evidence*
Home visitation and health worker outreach	Visits by community health workers or nurses to households	IPV	*Promising*	*Insufficient evidence*
Justice and law-enforcement interventions	Mobile courts, increased enforcement, the second response	IPV, NPSV	*Ineffective*	*Not applicable or no evidence*
Personnel training	Sensitisation, identification, or response training with institutional personnel (e.g., teachers, police officers, first responders, health professionals)	IPV, NPSA, FGM, CM	*Ineffective*	*Ineffective*
Infrastructure and transport	Improving the safety of public transport, street lighting	NPSA	*Insufficient evidence*	*Insufficient evidence*

Source: Adapted from: Ellsberg, Mary & Arango, Diana & Morton, Matthew & Gennari, Floriza & Kiplesund, Sveinung & Contreras, Manuel & Watts, Charlotte. (2014). Prevention of Violence against Women and Girls: What Does the Evidence Say?. The Lancet. http://dx.doi.org/10.1016/S0140-6736(14)61703-7

Note: Programmes will often incorporate multiple components and overlaps reflecting more than one intervention type. Presented results are based on trials, including randomized controlled trials (RCTs) or quasi-experimental trials with comparison groups. IPV=intimate partner violence. NPSA=non-partner sexual assault. FGM=female genital mutilation. CM=child marriage.

Findings by the category of violence

The two meta-analytic studies of the effectiveness of VAWG interventions (Arango et al., 2014; Ellsberg et al., 2014) provide a valuable overview of the findings of VAWG program effectiveness across different categories of violence and country income levels. Key findings from these overviews will be presented in the following paragraphs.

Intimate Partner Violence

A large number of impact evaluations (19 comprehensive and 15 systematic reviews) address IPV. The majority of interventions in this field took place in high-income countries and focused on secondary prevention approaches, namely:

1. batterer interventions (centred on men/perpetrators, generally lack positive effects on VAWG),
2. survivor services (centred on women/survivors, more mixed-results; in particular, intensive advocacy services and psychosocial support have positive results).

Evaluated interventions generally score as of moderate quality: sample sizes tended to be small; sampling strategies were unclear; there is a lack of data on the cost-effectiveness of interventions, and the impact of working in a multisectoral manner was not sufficiently measured.

Primary Prevention Interventions

Primary prevention refers to reducing the number of new instances of violence by intervening before violence takes place. These interventions involve fostering societies, communities, organizations, and relationships in which violence is less likely to occur (for example, by challenging attitudes, behaviours, and practices that justify, excuse, or condone violence).

Although primary prevention approaches have been much less frequently studied, encouraging results emerge from interventions in the middle- and low-income settings.

High-income countries: Four evaluations with positive findings include a Hawaiian program of perinatal home visiting, a reproductive coercion evaluation in California, and two group training programs on "Healthy Relationships" in Canada, conducted with male and female high school students or at-risk youth. The two Canadian programs showed significant reductions in dating violence perpetration in the intervention group compared to the control groups.

1. **Home visitations (HV)** have traditionally been used to monitor pregnancy, protect the health of pregnant women and infants, and improve parenting skills. Given their close contact with women, HV programs have the potential to reduce IPV, but limited evidence of their effectiveness is available so far. However, further research is urged in this field to make the role of home-visiting nurses more effective in IPV prevention.

   Main findings: During the implementation of Hawaii's Healthy Start Program (HSP) (Duggan et al., 1999), mothers in the intervention group reported significantly lower IPV victimisation rates than mothers in the control group.

1. **Advocacy**: Reproductive coercion includes pregnancy coercion (e.g. male partners' verbal pressure to get women

pregnant) and active interference with conceptive methods (birth control sabotage). It increases the risk of unintended pregnancy, HIV infection, and other sexual and reproductive health concerns.

<u>Main findings</u>: An intervention conducted in four family-planning clinics in Urban Northern California found a 71 per cent decrease in the odds of pregnancy coercion among women in the intervention group compared to participants in the control clinics. Women in the intervention arm were also more likely to report ending unhealthy relationships.

1. **School-based interventions**: There is good evidence that school-based interventions can prevent dating violence. The more effective and promising interventions had more extended programmes delivered by highly trained facilitators or teachers, used participatory learning approaches, including critical reflection and skills building, and were based on theories of gender and power. They were also evaluated with long-term follow-up. More research is needed to develop interventions to use more effectively in classrooms, especially in LMIC settings, and ensure the impact on girls and boys. (Kerr-Wilson, 2020).

1. **Working with men and boys only** (Kerr-Wilson, 2020): 1) participatory educational programmes that promote positive masculinity and 2) bystander interventions in schools and sports teams mainly applied in US universities.

Low- and Middle-Income Countries: The interventions focusing on the primary prevention of IPV use a wide range of approaches, including group training; social communication, such as radio and television spots, billboards, theatre, and so forth; community mobilization; and livelihood strategies.

1. **Group training for women and men**: Many of the interventions emerged from HIV programming, with the growing recognition of gender inequality and IPV as a driver of HIV infection.

Main findings: Stepping Stones, a program applied in 70 villages in South Africa, uses participatory learning approaches to build knowledge, risk awareness, and communication and relationship skills relating to gender, violence and HIV. Two years following an intervention, men's self-reported perpetration of physical and sexual IPV was significantly lower compared to men in the control villages (p=0.05). Still, no differences were found in women's reports of IPV victimization (Jewkes et al., 2008).

1. **Group training for men**: An intervention targeting both married and unmarried young men in Mumbai and Gorakhpur, India, aimed to reduce male-perpetrated VAWG by transforming gender-inequitable norms through group training and "social lifestyle marketing."

Main findings: Again, men's self-reported perpetration of physical and sexual IPV was significantly lower compared to participants in the comparison group (p<0.005).

1. **Working with men and boys only** (Kerr-Wilson, 2020): 1) participatory educational programmes that promote positive masculinity and 2) bystander interventions in schools and sports teams mainly applied in US universities. From the first approach, men's discussions groups in Côte d'Ivoire (Hossain

et al., 2014); interactive group education and community mobilisation with young men in Ethiopia (Pulerwitz et al., 2015) and India (Verma et al., 2008) showed good results in reducing IVP and NPSA.

1. **Couples' interventions and parenting programmes** (Kerr-Wilson, 2020): There is good evidence that well-designed, long-term and more intensive interventions, primarily when also addressing alcohol abuse, are an effective approach for reducing women's experiences of IPV.

1. **Livelihood programmes**: An innovative programme, IMAGE, applied in South Africa, combined microfinance with training and skills-building sessions on preventing HIV infection, gender norms, cultural beliefs, communication, and intimate partner violence. More recent intensive long-term programmes that combine economic and social empowerment components were found to reduce women's and girls' experience of physical, sexual and/or emotional violence (Kerr-Wilson, 2020).

Cork et al., 2018: Evaluations of microfinance/economic empowerment alone indicate that they do not suffice to decrease IPV-related measures and may increase controlling behaviours (Green et al., 2015; Gupta et al., 2013; Kim et al., 2009) and suggest that microfinance programmes should be accompanied by comprehensive couples training (Gupta et al., 2013).

<u>Main findings</u>: There was a reduction of over 50 per cent in women's reports of physical or sexual violence from a partner in the intervention group compared to the control group.

1. **Direct transfers of cash, food or food stamps** (Kerr-Wilson et al., 2020): Examples from South Africa, Ecuador and Bangladesh are mentioned above (see p. x)

Secondary Prevention Interventions

Secondary prevention involves the health and justice sector. It refers to both mitigating the immediate consequences of abuse by providing already-abused women and girls with services and supports (e.g. emergency contraception, post-exposure prophylactic-PEP, psychosocial support, and counselling), and also preventing recurrent or repeat abuse (e.g. through timely protection and safety for domestic violence survivors, removal of perpetrators from the household, and orders of protection) (Fergus, L., 2012).

Batterer intervention programs (BIP): Two systematic and one comprehensive reviews analysed the effects of court-mandated BIP in high-income settings. BIPs typically involve group education lasting from 8 to 24 weeks. One of the most well-known approaches is the "Duluth Model," a feminist approach that engages men in discussions about power and control. Other commonly used approaches are cognitive behavioural therapy (CBT) and anger management, both of which seek to change violent behaviour using established behavioural strategies, as well as discussions of thought patterns and beliefs (Smedslund et al., 2007). A few programmes tested new approaches, such as combining batterers' treatment with substance abuse programmes or applied racially and culturally adapted programs for specific groups.

<u>Main findings</u>: Although the authors of reviews on this type of intervention acknowledge the need for additional research, the meta-analysis conducted by Feder et al. (2008) does not provide strong

support for the effectiveness of BIPs in reducing violence recidivism among perpetrators. Overall, batterers' programs have very high dropout rates, and there are few consequences for not completing the program. Nevertheless, BIP can have potentially harmful effects on victims, especially when the cost of the court-mandated intervention is not subsidized.

The screening occurs through health services and involves pregnant women screened for violence during prenatal care. In situations of violence, health care providers can refer women to shelters, counselling or legal services. However, significant disagreement remains regarding the use of universal (which requires more time and resources) versus targeted screening.

Main findings: Evaluations of screening programs have found statistically-significant positive results for identifying survivors of IPV, but there is no evidence whether it was followed by increased referrals to support agencies. According to the reviews, screening itself was not harmful to women. The few screening evaluations that actually reported decreases in violence usually combined screening with psychosocial support or another type of survivor service. Several screening evaluations report positive outcomes for women and their children, such as decreased depression, lower stress, and greater knowledge and use of services.

Survivor services: "women-centred" programmes targeting known survivors or women newly identified through the screening. These interventions use a combination of strategies to provide women with resources to reduce their future risk of violence and improve their health status.

   a. **Psychosocial counselling**: may provide danger assessments, safety planning, and referrals to specialized services.

<u>Main findings</u>: A successful screening program in Hong Kong provided pregnant women with an "empowerment intervention" (consisting of advice in the area of safety, decision making, problem-solving, and an "empathic understanding" component derived from client-centred therapy).

a. **Advocacy interventions** include many of the same components as the psychosocial and home visitation programs. These programs provide additional support to women from a layperson/community trained in identifying and accessing services.

<u>Main findings</u>: An intensive community-based advocacy intervention for women leaving a battered women's shelter in Michigan trained lay advocates to help women access the community resources they needed to reduce their risk of future IPV. Women who worked with advocates over two years experienced significantly less violence (p=0.03), reported a higher quality of life and social support and had less difficulty obtaining community resources than women who did not receive such services.

Child Sexual Abuse

<u>Availability of evidence</u>: only one systematic review of the empirical evidence on the effectiveness of interventions addressing child sexual abuse was found in the World Bank report (Zwi et al., 2007). However, this review was rated high quality and offered important insights in this domain.

<u>Main findings</u>: The review examined the evidence for various school-based interventions and found no evidence that any of them

reduced victimisation or perpetration of child sexual abuse or led to greater access to services for sexually assaulted children. The only measured outcome that was found to be positively impacted in some of the interventions was increased knowledge by children on what constitutes abuse. However, it is not clear whether such knowledge would affect their behaviours. The review also found instances of adverse consequences from some interventions, such as nightmares, growth of peer violence, increased dependency, fearfulness of strangers, hesitation to go to school, etc. Although appearing in the minority of the interventions, such adverse effects illustrate the need to carefully assess all possible implications of interventions in the VAWG area.

Harmful Traditional Practices

<u>Availability of evidence</u>: Two reviews of HTP interventions were found in the literature, one assessed as a high-quality systematic review (Berg & Denison, 2012) and the other as a comprehensive review (Lee-Rife, Malhotra, Warner, & Glinski, 2012). The first review focused on interventions designed to reduce the victimisation or perpetration of FGM/C. Lee-Rife and colleagues (2012) review examined interventions or policies that had recorded measurement of change in behaviour, knowledge, or attitudes related to child marriage among relevant stakeholders. The authors of these reviews point out the overall scarcity of robust empirical evidence on the effectiveness of interventions in this area. Most impact evaluations focused on changes in attitudes towards the practice itself or on the intention of mothers to have their daughters endure the procedure in the future. Very few measured actual changes in instances of victimisation or perpetration of FGM/C or showed the empirical data that would allow for estimation of any kind of effect sizes. The reviewers especially emphasise the need to measure potential negative consequences of such HTP interventions, based on their findings that in some cases,

unintended consequences, such as the increased misconception that FGM/C is acceptable if performed as a medically safe procedure, could occur.

<u>Main findings</u>: Community mobilisation programmes, such as the TOSTAN model (named after its founding NGO), first used in Senegal and later expanded in several other sub-Saharan countries, have significantly reduced the prevalence of FGM/C practices in participating rural villages. The approach is based on community education programmes on health, literacy, human rights and other issues. An important aspect of the programme is that villagers themselves identify priority issues for community action, among which FGM/C and IPV were singled out as critical problems. A quasi-experimental evaluation of the programme showed a significant reduction of VAWG and instances of FGM/C practices. Notably, such decreases were reported even among the villagers not directly involved in the programme.

Group training for women and girls, sometimes used in the HTP interventions, has mixed results. The programmes that showed significant decreases in child marriages used a comprehensive set of activities, including intensive "life skills" training for unmarried girls, community discussions, mentorship, community service activities to encourage parents to keep girls in school, economic incentives, etc. In general, the overview of these interventions shows that programmes based on stand-alone interventions, such as awareness-raising and media advocacy campaigns, even when combined with legislative measures, do not tend to result in significant delays in child marriage. On the other hand, a well-thought community-based intervention that accounts for local cultural context and involves all key stakeholders, allowing their input and development of their sense of agency and ownership, can result in a significant decrease in HTP, even with relatively modest means (Lee-Rife et al., 2012)

Non-Partner Sexual Abuse

<u>Availability of evidence</u>: Among the reviews of sexual assault prevention programs, the most numerous were those focusing on the primary prevention of acquaintance-perpetrated sexual assault ("date-rape", particularly among North American university-level students), while there is a particular lack of rigorous evidence for interventions addressing workplace sexual harassment. Numerous impact evaluations found significant improvement in rape-related knowledge and attitudes, but only two of them reported decreased non-partner sexual assault itself. Most of the reviews focused on interventions implemented in high-income settings and generally scored as moderate quality (AMSTAR scale).

<u>Main findings</u>: Of 17 included intervention evaluations, only two reported significantly positive results in reducing non-partner sexual assault. Both interventions are university-based sexual assault prevention programs in the US, and it is not clear to what extent they could be meaningfully applied in different settings/populations. These programs consisted of training, video elements, discussion groups or role-playing activities (Anderson & Whiston, 2005). Their content included topics of risk-reduction, gender role socialization, or information and discussions on myths and facts about sexual assault.

Peer violence prevention intervention was studied mainly in HIC, and a small number of studies were conducted in Africa and South Asia. An example of self-defence training to prevent sexual assault is the EAAA programme applied in Canadian universities (Senn et al., 2015/2017).

Summary of empirical evidence

Change is possible

Presented evidence on the effectiveness of VAWG interventions clearly shows that change is possible, i.e. happening or reoccurring of VAWG is preventable. However, the presented findings also point out that positive change is by no means guaranteed. Therefore, programme initiators need to employ an approach adequate to the given situation, context, participants and types of violence to induce desired change.

In high-income countries, secondary interventions with the VAWG victims have often shown success in improving survivors' physical and mental health. On the other hand, evidence for their effectiveness in reducing the rates of revictimization is still weak. Considerable research has also been done about interventions designed to address perpetrators but with limited evidence of their effectiveness. In the LMIC context, the main focus of VAWG interventions is the prevention of various forms of violence. Assessment of these programmes indicates that it is possible to reduce the prevalence of violence, with some interventions reaching substantial positive effects within the timeframe of the programmes.

Evidence on 'what works' is growing but is still insufficient

Another highly positive development is that the evidence base is rapidly increasing, indicating that more solid evidence on what works and under which conditions will be available soon and will only expand over the coming decades. And more robust evidence is clearly needed! That is because interventions that bring targeted change are still an exception rather than a rule. Furthermore, persistent inconsistency of results across the studies (and even across different outcomes within a single study), and a vast heterogeneity of the interventions in many relevant aspects, leaves very little room for accurate generalisations of the findings. Even less so is possible to make reliable predictions on what kind of intervention would work in future and under which conditions.

Most interventions are ineffective (lead to no change)

The main, and probably most striking finding from this overview is that among selected VAWG interventions, more than two-thirds were found to have no effects on targeted outcomes (**Figure 17**). Half of the remaining interventions had mixed results. Only every tenth evaluated VAWG intervention had a significant positive effect! Furthermore, in 5% of cases, adverse effects of VAWG intervention are observed. For example, suppose we imagine a school class of 20 pupils. In that case, these results indicate that a particular course did not teach 14 students anything; it brought some insufficient knowledge to 3 students and helped 2 students to learn something from the presented material (to the unknown level or extent of understanding). It also incidentally made one of the students learn the wrong things in the process. Any school evaluation would undoubtedly find such results unsatisfactory or even catastrophic. They would indicate a massive amount of wasted resources of all stakeholders. Well, we come to the same conclusion here. Yes, the change is possible but is not easy to obtain. Why it is the case has something to do with the complexity of the problem (more on that below). But this review points out that the general inefficiency of the VAWG interventions is due to the interventions themselves. But before we examine the observed limitations in reviewed interventions and the gaps in available empirical evidence, we will outline some of the lessons learned from the few studies that have managed to achieve reductions in various forms of VAWG.

Figure 17: Impact assessment across selected studies by type of violence

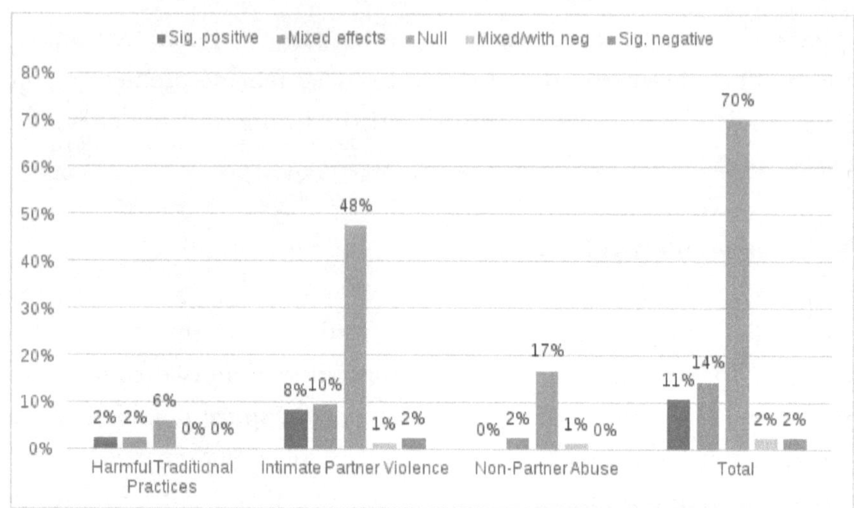

Source: Adjusted from Arango et al. (2014). Interventions to prevent or reduce violence against women and girls: A systematic review of reviews. http://dx.doi.org/10.13140/RG.2.1.2545.6168

Lessons learned

Due to relatively few cases of effective interventions and high heterogeneity across studies, only a few general patterns can be discerned from the reviewed findings. The following paragraphs briefly outline these common features across the successful VAWG interventions.

Multicomponent approaches work better

In general, interventions based on the multi-component approach, which engage multiple stakeholders and tackle several related aspects, tend to be more effective in preventing VAWG than single-component programmes. For example, micro-financing programmes are more effective when combined with gender equality training.

Addressing norms and power dynamics behind VAWG is crucial for programmes success

The review also shows that gender-transformative approaches addressing social norms and power dynamics behind VAWG are more likely to be effective than programmes targeting only attitude and behavioural change. This principle holds across different types of intervention approaches, including parenting programmes, economic interventions, or school-based interventions (Fulu et al., 2015; Dworkin et al., 2013).

Working with both women and men tends to give better results

Emerging evidence indicates that interventions that work with both men and women are more likely to be effective than those working with only women or only men. That is an important finding given that most VAWG interventions currently focus on working exclusively with women (e.g. economic empowerment interventions) or with boys and men (e.g. the majority of bystander interventions). Therefore, these aspects of interventions should be reconsidered, as evidence suggests that such segregation is not conducive to producing desired changes.

Face-to-face engagement is needed

It seems that face-to-face engagement with the target population is needed to achieve lasting behavioural or social change. For example, the Bell Bajao campaign[6] in India has reached millions of people through various traditional and social media channels. Still, its community outreach aspect seems to be the key to its success (Fulu et al., 2015). Of course, such a result is not unexpected since it aligns with empirical evidence from other social intervention programmes that consistently highlight the importance of personal connection and communication in inducing desired changes.

4. Gaps and limitations in empirical evidence

The complexity of the VAWG interventions

Before discussing limitations and gaps in the empirical evidence on what works in VAWG interventions, we will shortly discuss the complexity of the VAWG programmes and the many challenges they are facing in their quest for positive change. We have seen a great variety of VAWG intervention approaches, forms, topics, and characteristics and that they can have vastly different outcomes. But behind all this variety, one commonality shared among them is that it is generally challenging to prepare and organise them, and even more so to produce a measurable and lasting desired change. Reasons for this are many, including a multitude of the environmental and personal factors behind any occurrence of VAWG. But one of the critical aspects of any VAWG intervention is its embeddedness in a given social context and the consequent need for shaping an intervention to fit the given context accurately.

Proper understanding and accounting for a given context are critical for the positive outcome of any program intervention undertaken within a social setting. That is maybe even more valid when it comes to preventing VAGW. That is why successful interventions in this area are highly dependent on the proper understanding of the causes, forms and consequences of violence in a given social setting. Moreover, such a situation necessitates that even the same types of interventions (e.g. community mobilisation or group-based training) have to be prepared and implemented differently in different cultural contexts.

Several specific aspects of VAWG make monitoring and evaluating impact in this area particularly challenging, which points to the need for particular considerations when designing and implementing M&E for VAWG programs. In particular, VAWG closely interrelates with deeply entrenched social norms (values, beliefs, attitudes, behaviours and practices) and, therefore, can be particularly difficult to address. There are many barriers to overcome before impact is evident and lasting changes in behaviour or attitude may take a period of one generation to take root. Likewise, VAWG interventions frequently involve multiple strategies and focus areas, contributing to different outcomes and impacts. That is why a mixed-method approach that uses both quantitative and qualitative methodologies in evaluation is often more fitting here than in some other areas of policy evaluations. Tackling VAWG also requires a holistic approach more often than other policy areas. When seeking to transform social norms, it is necessary to work at both the individual and the collective level, addressing values, beliefs, attitudes, behaviours and practices in an integrated way.

A limited quantity of available empirical evidence

Although we now know more than ever before about what works to prevent VAWG, this knowledge is still somewhat limited and "more research is needed to improve our understanding of how different interventions work and for whom, and the synergies between them" (WHO, 2019). As we could see in previous sections, there are entire domains of VAWG with only a few empirical studies available globally, with IPV being the only form of violence attracting more substantive research attention. The limited quantity of empirical evidence and the vast heterogeneity in its quality and intervention characteristics has led the authors of all analysed systematic reviews to restrain from any kind of statistical meta-analysis (pooling of data). For example, the authors of the World Bank review expressly point out "that statistical meta-analysis (pooling of data) would be inappropriate and would lack credibility" (Arango et al., 2014; p. 13). They instead provide descriptive statistics to summarise the nature and scope of the reviewed evidence.

It is essential to distinguish two factors contributing to the lack of available empirical evidence on VAWG effectiveness. The first one is obvious and concerns the general scarcity of intervention programs in this area, especially in non-IPV forms of VAWG. Globally, until the last two decades, there were few such programmes. But then, they started to proliferate across the world in an uneven and *ad hoc* manner, highly dependent on unreliable and inconsistent sources of funding. With the strong growth of such programmes in recent years, the second factor emerges as the main limitation to the faster accumulation of quality empirical evidence this area badly needs. That second factor is the small proportion of VAWG intervention studies implementing robust impact assessment methodologies and, more generally, the accumulation of empirical evidence.

Although some exceptions exist, few VAWG programmes incorporate robust systems to monitor and evaluate their impact, and the current evidence base is weak. Reasons for that include the difficulty of obtaining reliable data, the complexity and context-specificity of VAWG interventions, and the political and social dynamics surrounding these issues. However, without assessing the intervention's impact and results, we lose an opportunity to build a critical evidence base and learn how change happens, restricting overall chances of preventing VAWG.

A good illustration of the paucity of VAWG interventions employing rigorous impact assessment approaches (if at all) is presented in the best meta-analysis so far – the World Bank's 2014 report (Arango et al., 2014). The authors have started their search with 3,687 identified reviews, among which only 23 systematic reviews satisfied Cochrane Handbook's standards (Green & Higgins, 2009). They further included 35 "comprehensive reviews", despite their methodological limitations and non-compliance with the standards, due to the importance of their findings and general scarcity of good quality systematic reviews. **Figure 18** presents the flow diagram explaining the study selection process applied in this study. As the authors note: "Lacking a predetermined systematic methodology, comprehensive reviews should generally be viewed as inherently more susceptible to bias in identifying and analysing evidence than would systematic reviews" (Arango et al., 2014, p. 15).

Figure 18: Selection of review papers in Arango et al. (2014)

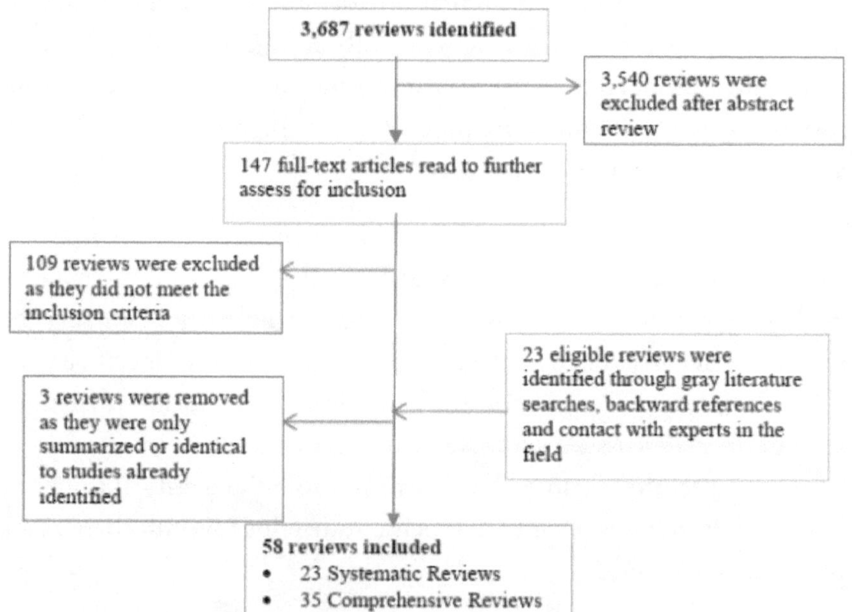

Source: Arango, Diana & Morton, Matthew & Gennari, Floriza & Kiplesund, Sveinung & Ellsberg, Mary. (2014). Interventions to prevent or reduce violence against women and girls: A systematic review of reviews. http://dx.doi.org/10.13140/RG.2.1.2545.6168

Furthermore, of the 290 intervention studies included in the 58 selected reviews (23 systematic and 35 comprehensive), only 84 (29%) offered information on the impact assessment of VAGW outcomes. Other studies either had no information on VAGW outcomes, i.e. lacked experimental or quasi-experimental design, or did not provide sufficient information on the effect of the tested intervention. The flow diagram (**Figure 19**) presents the selection of individual impact assessment studies used in the World Bank's report.

Figure 19: Selection of individual impact evaluation studies in Arango et al. (2014)

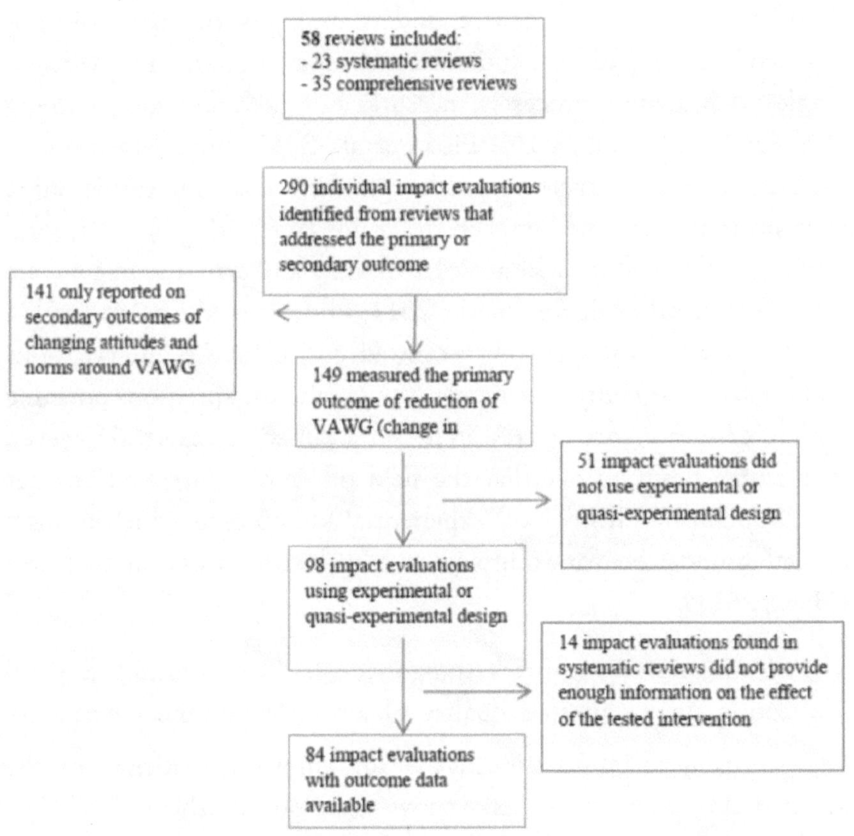

Source: Arango, Diana & Morton, Matthew & Gennari, Floriza & Kiplesund, Sveinung & Ellsberg, Mary. (2014). Interventions to prevent or reduce violence against women and girls: A systematic review of reviews. http://dx.doi.org/ 10.13140/RG.2.1.2545.6168

Limited quality of empirical evidence

A limited quantity of the available empirical evidence on the effectiveness of VAWG interventions is not the only constraint. Unfortunately, even the obtained evidence has some serious flaws and limitations that affect its quality and, consequently, its usability. For example, reviewed studies have generally relied on single-factor solutions, offered a poor general understanding of the mechanism of targeted change, and have limited consistency, rigour, and quality of employed evaluation processes, measures and methodologies (Ellsberg et al., 2014; Florquin, 2016; Picon et al., 2017; Bott, Morrison, & Ellsberg, 2005). Furthermore, although there is an increasing effort to evaluate programmes' impact, the teams conducting interventions, unfortunately, tend to lack the skills, funding and expertise to generate robust empirical evidence (Heise, 2011, Ellsberg et al., 2014). Such a situation reflects the relatively recent advent of VAWG interventions and the fact that many individuals, groups, and organisations pursuing such interventions are not researchers or evaluation experts. However, it is worth pointing out that the field of VAWG interventions has a well-established history of "experiential knowledge", which forms a critical foundation for future impact evaluation work in this area (Heise, 2011).

The World Bank's report (Arango et al., 2014) brings a good illustration of the limited quality of available evidence. A quality analysis using AMSTAR ratings[7] for empirical evidence of the selected 23 systematic reviews shows that one of them is of "low quality", 10 are of "moderate quality", and 12 are of "high quality". Overall, the authors identified substantial heterogeneity in the quality of the selected reviews. The additional cause of concern was that some of the reviews that included a more significant number of studies were of inferior quality.

The meta-analysis of Pundir and colleagues (2020) in the domain of IPV interventions shows similar heterogeneity in the quality of identified impact assessment studies, with the majority of them being of "medium" or "low" confidence (**Figure 20**).

Figure 20: Number of systematic reviews by study confidence

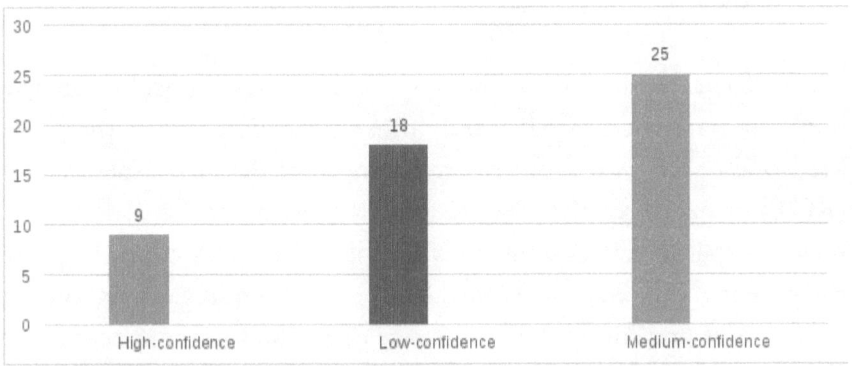

Source: Pundir P, Saran A, White H, Subrahmanian R, Adona J. (2020).

Another good illustration of the limiting quality of existing empirical evidence in this area is research carried out among the practitioners of VAWG interventions (Florquin, 2016). In an online survey, these respondents overwhelmingly reported the perceived need for better measurement of the impact of VAWG interventions. In particular, respondents were asked to rate their level of agreement with the following statement: "there is a need to better measure the problem of GBV [gender-based violence] during emergencies in order to understand the true extent of the problem". Practitioners of VAWG interventions and humanitarian workers had a mean agreement score of 85 and 90 out of 100, respectively.

In the following paragraphs, we will shortly outline a list of methodological and procedural weaknesses that have impaired the quality of available evidence in the VAWG area. The overview is not exhaustive, and it does not offer an in-detail analysis of such limitations or gaps, as that would be out of the scope of this report. Instead, the overview aims to inform the interested reader about the main aspects of quality limitations that should be considered when evaluating available empirical evidence on the effectiveness of VAWG interventions.

Risk of bias

Most of the meta-analyses and systematic reviews consulted in the literature have tried to select only those evaluation studies that have used one of the two more rigorous empirical designs: experimental (RCT) or quasi-experimental designs. The reasoning for such criteria is clear: experimental designs allow for the best possible control against the potential influence of external factors (confounding effects) on the results, thus preventing the occurrence of any bias in the outcomes of the interventions.

However, the problem remains that even the few identified studies that used experimental, randomised-control trials did not necessarily employ the complete experimental protocols in their studies. And any case in which experimental protocol is not adhered to is a potential source of bias in studies' findings.

A good illustration of the shortcomings of the employed RCTs in IPV interventions is presented in the study of Cork and colleagues (2018). **Figure 21** summarises the "risks of bias" across various aspects of experimental design for the RCT studies they identified (their focus was on IPV studies conducted in Sub-Saharan Africa). They identified multiple "high bias risk" and "unclear bias risk" aspects of evaluated experimental studies. The main bias treats are related to the lack of blinding of participants and personnel (performance bias) and the lack of blinding of outcome assessment (detection bias). These and other identified deficiencies are all associated with exaggerated estimates of intervention effects, casting doubt on the validity of the obtained findings even from the studies that have implemented the strongest impact assessment frameworks (Cork et al., 2018; Pildal et al., 2007; Portal, Bonet, & Cobo, 2007). Such exaggerated results are especially likely in those cases where outcome measures are based on subjective reports (e.g. attitudinal measures) rather than on objective markers, such as the prevalence of certain observable behaviours (Wood et al., 2008).

Figure 21: Risk of bias across various aspects of experimental design of identified RCT studies

88 | DR. MILOS KANKARAS

Author (Publication year)	Random sequence generation (selection bias)	Allocation concealment (selection bias)	Blinding of participants and personnel (performance bias)	Blinding of outcome assessment (detection bias)	Incomplete outcome data (attrition bias)	Selective reporting (reporting bias)
Abramsky et al. (2014)						
Falb et al. (2015)						
Green et al. (2015)						
Gupta et al. (2013)						
Hossain et al. (2014)						
Jewkes et al. (2008)						
Jones et al. (2013)						
Kim et al. (2009)						
Kyegombe et al. (2014)						
L'Engle et al. (2014)						
Minnis et al. (2015)						
Parcesepe et al. (2016)						
Pronyk et al. (2006)						
Wagman et al. (2015)						
Wechsberg et al. (2013)						

Source: Cork, C., White, R.G., Noel, P., Bergin, N. (2018); https://doi.org/10.1177/1524838018784585

Note: Red= High risk; Green= Low risk; Amber= Unclear risk

Inconsistent & conflicting evidence

Current evidence shows no single intervention approach with consistently positive empirical evidence on the effectiveness of VAWG interventions. In other words, even within those approaches where various individual interventions show a positive impact, there is a certain number of studies with no impact or even with negative impact. As Fulu and colleagues point out: "We are yet to see an intervention that has effectively reduced both men's perpetration and women's experiences of violence at the same time, with evaluations tending to report a change in one, but not in the other". This inconsistency does not occur only across the studies. It is also present within the individual studies. When a study reviews different types of outcomes (e.g. various forms of VAWG), the results vary across these outcomes, in some cases even bringing opposing effects (Fulu et al., 2015; Arango et al., 2014).

Furthermore, even when a single outcome is measured through two separate indicators, results can lead to disparate and sometimes contradictory findings. For example, in a study of IPV in Durban, South Africa, men (as potential perpetrators of violence) reported a significant decrease in IPV incidences. Yet, the women-reported incidence of IPV remained much the same (Crawford et al., 2020). Such high levels of inconsistency reflect the vast heterogeneity of VAWG interventions' characteristics, a general lack of fundamental understanding of the underlying mechanism of change and the factors that promote or hinder such change.

Lack of methodological rigour & high variability in the quality of impact assessment

A general lack of methodological rigour in the impact evaluation studies is reflected in all aspects of the research process. The approach to gathering data, measuring significant indicators, research design features, data analysis, and interpolation based on observed results vary considerably across studies (Kerr-Wilson et al., 2020; Arango et al., 2014). Many studies did not employ the best scientific practices, resorting instead to various *ad hoc* solutions, often not documented and reflected in the interpretation of final findings. For example, many studies used individual-level analysis for cluster RCTs with very few clusters. Others did not adjust to key baseline covariates in their analyses (Kerr-Wilson et al., 2020). Some studies reported a large number of associations without prior planning of their examination and without applying necessary statistical corrections to their p-values before interpreting them.[8] Another common limitation across the studies was the lack of proper information on report findings, effect sizes and confidence measures (Kerr-Wilson et al., 2020; Arango et al., 2014).

Small target groups (Lack of statistical power)

One of the persistent methodological limitations of many reviewed studies was the relatively small sample sizes of their target and control groups. That often led to studies not having enough statistical power to find even substantial effect sizes. Studies employing cluster RCTs have particularly often faced this problem, which severely limited their ability to reach reliable conclusions on the effectiveness of their interventions (Kerr-Wilson et al., 2020).

The reason behind small sample sizes often lies in limited resources available to the programme teams. Furthermore, this is often combined with their general lack of research expertise and understanding of the consequences of small sample sizes on their ability to draw clear conclusions on the workings of their interventions. On the other hand, small-sample impact assessment studies are often a stepping stone to the more extensive studies building upon the insights and positive indications provided in previous, smaller studies (Fulu et al., 2015).

Lack of standardised measures of VAWG outcomes

Another methodological limitation of the VAWG studies is their lack of standardised outcome measures. Instead, VAWG is assessed in myriad ways, which often rely on the response to a single question (Kerr-Wilson et al., 2020). Such measures are notoriously unreliable and often fail to capture the true prevalence of VAWG in the target population. What is more, such measurement noise reduces researchers' ability to detect the actual effects of their interventions, thus biasing their effectiveness findings. Also, diversified outcome measures limit the comparability and the generalisability of results across studies.

Lack of process monitoring and evaluation

Although impact assessment studies often focus exclusively on the outcome measures of their interventions, it is equally illuminating and helpful to track the quality of intervention services delivered in a given programme. For example, in the above-mentioned survey of the practitioners of VAWG interventions, one of the key insights was their reported complaint about the overemphasis on the final outputs. At the same time, little attention is placed on the quality of the provided services (Florquine, 2016). Therefore, evaluating the processes and quality of intervention delivery would ensure a better understanding of such interventions' positive and negative outcomes. It would also provide meaningful learning about the nature of the problem, potential mechanisms of its change, and various risk and mitigating factors. That is why future VAWG interventions should start paying more attention to the process evaluation of their interventions.

Few studies measure the impact on VAWG

Most of the reviewed programmes do not measure rates of VAWG as their outcome criteria (Fulu et al., 2015). Instead, they often focus on various "risk factors" and other indirect or intermediary outcome measures, such as attitudes, school attendance, parenting styles, sexual practices, etc. This tendency is mainly reflected in an overreliance on attitudinal measures as behavioural proxies, with a usually implicit assumption that changes in measured attitudes are automatically reflected in related behavioural changes. Consequently, most studies reporting positive effects are based on the significant change in these indirect outcomes. Far fewer studies show a substantial impact on reducing factual incidence rates and women's experiences of VAWG (Fulu et al., 2015). This important limitation should be kept in mind when interpreting the results since changes in indirect measures do not necessarily generate changes in actual VAWG incidence rates. That is not to say that such measures should be abandoned but rather that they should not be used as proxies of proper behavioural changes. Further, they should be interpreted in line with what they are, rather than what a researcher wants them to be in the absence of (changes in) better measures.

Lack of evaluation standards

Various methodological fallacies mentioned in the preceding paragraphs are due to the lack of willingness of the programme teams to implement evaluation standards and limited means and resources to fully or partially implement these standards. However, although general evaluation standards exist for intervention studies, there is still no common set of evaluation guidelines, principles and "best practices" developed in the VAWG area (Kerr-Wilson, 2020). That is not surprising, given the recency of the empirical field and the fact that most of the programmes still do not hire experienced researchers. One way to improve the generated empirical evidence would be to develop the standards and principles relying on the broader scientific standards yet offering customised solutions, guidelines and practices based on the growing number of experiences and insights from the current wave of studies. For example, DFID's (2012) guidance is a good attempt to contribute to this cause.

Gaps in the scope of empirical evidence

Apart from the limited quantity of available empirical evidence and the above-listed quality issues of the existing evidence, there are additional critical gaps in existing empirical data that severely limit its usability and generalisability. In the following paragraphs, we will outline some of the key evidence gaps in this area.

Limited evidence from LMIC

Empirical research on the effectiveness of VAWG interventions is significantly less robust in the LMIC contexts (Arango et al., 2014; Fulu et al., 2015; Picon et al., 2017; Kerr-Wilson et al., 2020). Of course, unequal distribution of evidence is a problem in its own right. Yet, it is especially worrisome because the regions with the highest prevalence of VAWG (South Asia, Middle East and North Africa, and Sub-Saharan Africa) also have the lowest rates of good quality impact assessment studies (Arango et al., 2014). Furthermore, vast differences in socio-economic situations in HICs and LMICs cast severe doubts about the transferability of the findings from high-income countries to the low- and middle-income contexts (Kerr-Wilson, 2020). This situation implies an urgent need to pour more resources into rigorous evaluations of intervention programs in low- and middle-income countries worldwide (Heise, 2011).

Unequal evidence across different intervention types

Good-quality empirical evidence on what works is generally scarce. However, there is a considerable difference in the amount of conducted research across different areas of VAWG. For example, micro-finance, school-based, relationship-level, and parenting interventions have built a much larger evidence base than complex and multi-component programmes to transform masculinities or change social norms (Fulu et al., 2015). Likewise, while most VAWG programmes focus on intimate partner violence, very few interventions evaluated the effectiveness of programmes aiming to prevent trafficking or child sexual abuse.

Even less evidence on vulnerable groups and intersectoral approach

Another imbalance in the available evidence is related to target populations. Most of the assessed VAWG interventions were conducted focusing on broader population groups of women, men and children, with little or no regard to the intersectionality of various disadvantages. That has resulted in minimal evidence on the effectiveness of intervention programmes for particularly vulnerable groups of women and girls. Such groups include the LGBT population, people living with disabilities, chronic illness, people belonging to ethnic or religious minorities, etc. (Fulu et al., 2015; Picon et al., 2017; Kerr-Wilson et al., 2020). This lack of evidence is especially worrisome because studies showed that women and girls from vulnerable groups are more likely to experience VAWG (Kerr-Wilson et al., 2015). Furthermore, the lack of intersectional approaches to VAWG research means very little knowledge of how various risk factors and disadvantages interact with VAWG incidences. That limits the programmes' ability to compile and implement more targeted and effective interventions for the vulnerable groups of women and girls that might need them the most.

Limited evidence from conflict and severely deprived areas

Like with vulnerable groups, there is very little usable empirical evidence on VAWG intervention effectiveness coming from severely deprived or conflict areas (Kerr-Wilson et al., 2020). In this case, again, the knowledge gap exists in the area where such knowledge is especially needed, as rates of VAWG tend to be substantially higher in conflict and post-conflict populations. That is because of precarious conditions, including higher poverty levels, worse mental health, the enduring impact of war, disrupted social networks, etc. Furthermore, in general, interventions in conflict areas are less effective at preventing VAWG than those administered in more stable settings. In such a situation, women and girls who need help the most tend to get it the least, and we know very little about how to help them effectively (Murphy et al., 2019). Finally, it should be noted that particularly fragile contexts are not constrained only to conflict-affected areas. Other forms of state fragility, such as corruption, authoritarianism, lack of institutions, economic collapse, natural disasters, etc., adversely affect levels of violence in numerous ways, implying the need for a different type of intervention strategy and form (Heise, 2011). Unfortunately, we currently know little to none about the effectiveness of various approaches to VAWG in such situations.

Lack of generalisability to broader population(s)

As discussed, few impact assessment studies employed actual incidence of violence as an outcome measure. And studies that did so measured the direct impact on violence almost exclusively among programme participants or their partners. In other words, very few evaluations assessed the impact on VAWG at the broader community or population levels (Fulu et al., 2015). That is problematic in many ways. Firstly, we are not sure about the scope of impact of any given programme, even though many of the programmes assume generalisability of their findings to a much broader population than direct participants in their sample. Not knowing how far-reaching are the effects also impairs the possibility of calculating the cost-effectiveness of interventions or comparing the intervention approaches in terms of their value for money. Finally, a lack of information on the scope of effect also impairs the scalability of the interventions and leaves them susceptible to significant inefficiencies and missed opportunities.

Lack of scalability to other contexts

Another constraint of the great majority of evaluated interventions is their lack of information on the potential scalability of any given intervention to other similar or distinct contexts. Such information would be hugely valuable in cases of programmes with proven effectiveness, especially in an area in which such programmes are so rare. However, most of the programmes exclusively focus on the impact of their intervention in a given context and for a given respondent group, offering little consideration to the potential generalisability of their findings across different settings. That is somewhat understandable given the general scarcity of robust empirical evidence in this area and the need for researchers first to establish "what works" in one setting before exploring its applicability in other contexts. Moreover, VAWG interventions are highly dependent on a given social context and, as such, are not straightforwardly applicable to even similar cultural contexts without further research.

Lack of interventions targeting institutional change

The great majority of VAWG interventions focus on either individuals, groups or communities, with only a few evaluating programmes that specifically target changes in formal and informal institutions (Picon et al., 2017). For example, in one of the reviewed meta-analyses, only two studies evaluated the impact of interventions focusing on the enforcement of existing laws or specific social norms linked to IPV (Picon et al., 2017). Moreover, although community- or system-level interventions often incorporate activities with local leaders or promote changed gender norms, the specific effects of these formal and informal institutional factors are mainly absent from the empirical evidence.

Lack of assessment of intervention intensity

Most studies focus on detecting any change in targeted outcome(s) given a specific (and often fixed) intervention approach. Such empirical design entails a somewhat limited understanding of the relationship between intervention and its outcome. In particular, one of the main limitations of this design is that we know little about the relationship between intervention intensity and changes in desired results. For example, researchers might find a given 1-week group training largely ineffective. However, it is not sure if the same group training would show better effects if administered over one month and, if it would, how significant the improvement would be. Indeed, in the few cases where intensity in interventions was varied, outcomes often changed, with increased intensity leading to stronger impact. For example, a school-based intervention in India was found to have a stronger effect on boys' attitudes after two years than after only one year (Fulu et al., 2015).

Lack of information on the effects of intervention's intensity also impairs the determination of the optimal intensity of the intervention. This further limits the cost-benefit calculations in intervention design and can severely damage the effectiveness of the study on its own and in comparison with other competing approaches. For example, although one-to-one programmes with pregnant women in HICs have shown a significant reduction in IPV incidence, such programmes would be rather costly and thus rarely available in LMIC contexts (Fulu et al., 2015). Therefore, it would be valuable to know the optimal duration of such programmes in LMICs to achieve the most significant impact within a shorter period, which is likely more feasible in these settings.

Lack of long-term impact assessments

Another essential evidence gap in existing evaluation studies is the duration of assessed impact. Most studies implement a short follow-up and measure only short-term outcomes, either right after the intervention or within six months (Kerr-Wilson et al., 2020; Fulu et al., 2015). That is problematic as most of the interventions have long-term rather than short-term objectives, which means that they cannot properly evaluate the effectiveness of their programmes based on the assessed short-term outcomes. Another, more critical problem with this strategy is that long-term outcomes are always more challenging to achieve than short-term ones. For example, two cash-transfer studies found that initial positive impacts were not sustained over more extended periods (Fulu et al., 2015)[9]. That means that the observed positive impacts identified in the minority of VAWG interventions are almost exclusively short-term impacts, not necessarily sustained over the middle- to longer-term periods. Moreover, short-term outcomes are more susceptible to various methodological limitations, such as social desirability, lack of blinding protocols, etc. These factors are further reasons for cautious interpretation of any positive impacts only based on short-term outcomes.

Lack of knowledge of the mechanism in which intervention works

Most of the VAWG impact assessment studies generally place little emphasis on the identification of crucial mediators and moderators of the relationship between their intervention and the target outcome. Consequently, there is little solid evidence on the intervention mechanism and the process through which desired change is generated and sustained. Furthermore, widespread "conflicting" evidence among the programmes implementing similar strategies suggests poorly understood change pathways. Such a situation also implies that cultural and socio-economic context plays a huge role and requires proper implementation in the design of any intervention (Fulu et al., 2015). Lack of knowledge of the change mechanism presents a massive obstacle to designing adequate studies. It means that even those interventions that are found to be effective in one context or time might be ineffective elsewhere or at another moment due to the variation in critical determinants unknown to programme teams.

Lack of studies examining the cost-effectiveness

Very few evaluated interventions implemented cost-effectiveness analysis. That is a severe limitation in the field, given often limited resources available for these interventions, especially in LMIC contexts. Cost-effectiveness evaluations would allow researchers and practitioners to compare different intervention strategies and aspects of individual approaches, such as intensities, target populations, intervention formats (e.g. online vs in-person), etc. In general, the entire field of VAWG interventions would greatly benefit from an increased focus on the cost-effectiveness of these programmes, especially in a situation where so few programmes are found to have desired effects.

Need for cautious interpretation of meta-analytic evidence

Before proceeding to the concluding discussion, it is worth briefly noting a few important points that need to be taken into account when interpreting the presented results of the meta-analytic evidence of the effectiveness of VAWG interventions.

Unanticipated consequences

Unanticipated consequences, both positive and negative, are potential outcomes of all intervention programs. In the VAWG domain, it is imperative to track them given the sensitivity of the topic and the vulnerability of the VAWG victims. One of the well-documented unintended consequences of VAWG programmes is the initial rise in reported sexual violence cases rather than their immediate reduction (DFID, 2012). For example, 8000 cases of sexual violence were reported in Nicaragua in 1997, compared to around 3000 in 1995. In the intermediary period between 1995-1997, special police stations for women opened, and extensive media awareness campaigns were launched. In general, data from 39 countries worldwide show that an increase of female police officers increases the number of reported sexual assaults. Such situations are not necessarily wrong, as they can indicate an increase in reporting of otherwise hidden instances of VAWG, which could finally be addressed appropriately. But they also show that programme impacts should be interpreted with care and in-depth understanding of the issues, rather than with overreliance on quantitative indicators of various outcomes.

Selection bias

When interpreting the results of the impact assessment studies of VAWG interventions, one also needs to consider that most VAWG interventions are implemented without any or with only limited evaluation of their impact (see section x). Furthermore, the studies that did apply more rigorous impact assessment designs and were thus included in identified systematic reviews of evidence are by no means representative subsamples of the entire field of VAWG interventions. On the other hand, the very fact that they implemented rigorous impact assessment sets them apart from the vast majority of interventions that did not apply such assessment. For one, they have dedicated resources to administer the assessment, which is a resource-intensive activity requiring separate control groups and several other conditions. Also, they have the internal expertise to develop a proper research design, implement the required methodology and analyse empirical data, already indicating a higher level of team capacity than what might be the case with teams who do not implement impact assessment. Finally, implemented impact assessment also implies that the programme team more thoroughly planned the intervention. For example, they probably drafted at least a rudimentary theory of change and consulted relevant conceptual and empirical works in the field.

One could imagine many other ways the minority of VAWG programmes with impact assessment might differ from those that did not do it. The main point here, it is very likely that the subsample of VAWG interventions that evaluated their impact is probably substantially different from those interventions that did not do so. In research methodology, this situation is called "selection bias" and is considered one of the critical threats to the validity of results achieved from such a sample. Following the common-sense approach, we could assume that selected studies are probably of better quality than unselected ones, for the very fact that they have achieved implementation of a rather rigorous impact assessment design. They are probably more resourceful, systematic, comprehensive, well-prepared, etc. But the truth is that we are not sure to which degree this is the case and thus cannot estimate the degree of bias in the presented data. We can just assume that the effectiveness of the selected programmes is probably better than the effectiveness of the programmes that haven't applied any impact assessment and were thus not reviewed in any of the meta-analyses. That is why the actual proportion of "effective" studies might be lower than the one presented in this overview and why these results should be taken as probably positively biased to some degree.

The fragility of statistically significant results

When evaluating quantitative results, it is important to remember that statistically significant results indicating only modest effect sizes are relatively unstable (might not appear in retesting under the same conditions) (Walsh et al., 2014). That means that substantive interpretation of the effectiveness of any particular intervention should not be based on simple "counting" of statistically positive or adverse effects. Instead, a broader set of statistical information and methodological considerations should be considered when making sense of quantitative findings. For example, one needs to take into account the following: available sample size and consequent statistical power, the type of (experimental) design, possible confounding factors that were and were not controlled, follow-up periods, type and reliability of outcome measures, social and cultural context, and many other aspects of a particular intervention programme. Some of the considered systematic reviews recognised this aspect well, resorting to a narrative summation of the available empirical evidence (e.g., Arango et al., 2014; Ellsberg et al., 2014). Others put more weight on the statistical significance, although still explicitly or implicitly acknowledging its shortcomings (Kerr-Wilson et al., 2020; Fulu et al., 2015). Anyway, the analysis of the presented evidence shows that there is much more in the evaluated data than what is captured by statistical significance measures. Overlooking this additional information would be a missed opportunity.

Limitations of this review

This rapid examination of the available empirical evidence is not a systematic review, and it does not aim to account for all impact assessments of VAWG interventions ever done. Instead, the report summarises the bulk of empirical evidence, primarily sourced from the experimental and quasi-experimental quantitative impact assessment studies. Sourced literature comes from academic journals and policy reports ("grey literature") issued worldwide. The source of the evaluated evidence is five major systematic reviews identified in this area, each relying on the published reviews and reports. That means those studies that have not published their findings are not included in this report, even though they might have achieved significant results.

That also means that many studies that applied only qualitative evaluation methods are not evaluated in this report. Our literature search was primarily focused on English-language publications, although we searched for the relevant literature in French, Spanish, and Portuguese. Due to the limitations in the applied methodological designs and considerable heterogeneity of the study characteristics, it was impossible to generate quantitative estimations of effect sizes across various intervention strategies and outcomes. Consequently, we had to resort to a mostly narrative description of the direction and scope of empirical evidence across multiple categories of data.

Summary

Violence against women and girls (VAWG) is a global health and wellbeing concern and a human rights violation. It is estimated that about one-third of women worldwide experience some form of VAWG at some point in their lives, with this proportion reaching two thirds in some countries (WHO, 2013). VAWG has severe detrimental consequences for its victims, including homicide, suicide, injuries, unintended pregnancies, mental health problems, etc. VAWG also impacts the broader community, as affected women are less likely to participate in regular activities, have reduced capacity to care for themselves and their children, work, and use available economic opportunities (International Rescue Committee, 2012).

VAWG is preventable. That is why there has been increasing policy attention to this issue in recent years, resulting in a growing number of VAWG intervention programmes implemented worldwide. These programmes are also increasingly informed by the emerging academic and policy research on the causes, related factors and consequences of VAWG. VAWG intervention programs aim to reduce the risks of various forms of VAWG occurring or repeating and provide support to VAWG victims. However, developing and implementing an effective VAWG prevention intervention is not easy. It requires a good understanding of the nature of the problem, the cultural and socio-economic context in which it occurs, and the underlying drivers, risks and mitigating factors that affect the likelihood of VAWG occurrence.

The degree to which VAWG interventions achieve their aims is the question asked in impact evaluation studies empirically evaluating programme outcomes. They mostly do so by comparing target outcomes between the group that received the intervention and a control group using experimental and quasi-experimental methods. Impact evaluation studies are critical for gathering empirical evidence on what kind of interventions work, for whom, under which conditions, for which outcomes and through which mechanisms. Such empirical insights can then be used in future VAWG interventions to avoid inefficient approaches, build on identified positive aspects, fine-tune the methodological design and thus significantly improve chances for achieving desired positive change.

In this report, we provide a general overview of the globally available empirical evidence on the effectiveness of VAWG intervention programs. First, we describe the types of conducted VAWG programmes, their prevalence and their main characteristics. We then examine findings concerning the effectiveness of these interventions, summarised across different intervention approaches and different forms of VAWG. Finally, we analyse the quality and quantity of the reviewed empirical evidence on VAWG programmes' effectiveness and discuss some of the critical gaps identified in this evidence.

The report primarily focuses on the findings presented in several systematic reviews that evaluated results from impact evaluation studies on various forms of VAWG. The reviewed evidence is gathered in high-income countries (HIC) and low- and middle-income countries (LMIC). It is based on studies implementing experimental or quasi-experimental designs and systematically measuring their target outcomes. The evidence comprises studies on harmful traditional practices, intimate partner violence, non-partner sexual assaults, trafficking, child sexual abuse, and peer violence. Reviewed studies implement various intervention approaches, including individual-level interventions, group-based training, economic empowerment, community mobilisation, system-wide multi-component strategies, etc.

The **main findings** of our review are the following:

Few VAWG interventions employ robust impact assessment

Unfortunately, only a minority of VAWG programmes have incorporated robust systems to monitor and evaluate their impact, resulting in a relatively limited amount of available empirical evidence on their effectiveness. That might be due to many factors, such as the difficulty of obtaining reliable data, the complexity and context-specificity of VAWG interventions, and the political and social dynamics surrounding these issues. Nevertheless, by assessing impact and results, we have an opportunity to build a critical evidence base and to learn how change happens, contributing to overall efforts to prevent VAWG.

The number of impact assessment studies in the VAWG field is rapidly growing

One very encouraging development is that the evidence base has rapidly increased in recent years and is expected to further expand in the future. That means that we can expect more solid evidence on what works and under which conditions over the coming decades.

Positive change through VAWG interventions is possible

Analysis of the effectiveness of VAWG interventions confirms that change is possible, i.e. occurring or reoccurring VAWG is preventable. However, the presented findings also point out that positive change is by no means guaranteed or even the most likely intervention outcome. In high-income countries, secondary interventions with the VAWG victims have often shown success in improving survivors' physical and mental health. On the other hand, evidence of their effectiveness in reducing the rates of revictimization is still weak. Considerable research has also been done about interventions designed to address perpetrators, but the evidence of their effectiveness is limited. In the

LMIC context, the main focus of VAWG interventions is the prevention of various forms of violence. Assessment of these programmes indicates that it is possible to reduce the prevalence of violence, with some interventions reaching substantial positive effects within the timeframe of the programmes.

Most of the VAWG interventions have limited to no positive impact

More robust evidence is dearly needed since the current evidence base is still relatively weak and inconclusive. The main, and probably most striking finding from this overview is that among selected VAWG interventions, more than two-thirds were found to have no effects on targeted outcomes (**Figure 1**). Half of the remaining interventions had mixed results. Only every tenth evaluated VAWG intervention had a significant positive impact! Furthermore, in 5% of cases, adverse effects of VAWG intervention are observed.

Some VAWG interventions have negative consequences

Unfortunately, findings suggest that some interventions have had unintended negative consequences on some outcomes. Although the proportion of such programmes was relatively small, such findings point out the need for careful planning of intervention programmes to minimise the risks of such events occurring. But they also indicate how important it is to conduct impact evaluations of all VAWG intervention programs to provide an opportunity for all practitioners and researchers in the VAWG field to learn what works and what doesn't and to use such knowledge in the future interventions.

The quality of available empirical evidence is generally poor

Unfortunately, the existing evidence on the effectiveness of VAWG programmes has several serious flaws and limitations that affect its quality and, consequently, its usability. Reviewed studies are characterised by limited consistency, rigour, and quality of employed evaluation processes, measures and methodologies. They also often based their intervention on a poor general understanding of the mechanism of targeted change and involved risk factors and potential moderators of intervention effects. In addition, the impact assessment was often conducted with relatively small sample sizes, not using reliable outcome measures, and with a focus on various indirect measures of VAWG rather than its actual incidences in the target population. Furthermore, although there is an increasing effort to evaluate programmes' impact, the teams conducting interventions often lack the skills, funding, and expertise to generate robust empirical evidence. As a result, obtained empirical results, even in cases where the impact was assessed as positive, have to be interpreted with caution and care, taking into account specific methodological constraints ingrained within each particular study design.

Evidence gaps are many

There are many critical gaps in existing empirical data on the effectiveness of VAWG interventions that severely limit the usability and generalisability of its findings. In the following paragraphs, we will outline some of the key evidence gaps in this area. 1) First of all, there is much less robust empirical research on the effectiveness of VAWG interventions coming from LMIC contexts. 2) There is a considerable difference in the amount of conducted studies across different research areas. Some areas, such as micro-finance interventions, receive much more attention than complex and multi-component programmes to transform system-level discrimination or change social norms. 3) Limited evidence exists on the effectiveness of intervention programmes with particularly vulnerable groups of women and girls, such as LGBT populations, people living with disabilities, chronic illness, people belonging to various ethnic or religious minorities, etc. 4) There is very little usable empirical evidence on VAWG intervention effectiveness coming from severely deprived or conflict regions. 5) Very few evaluations assessed the impact on VAWG beyond their respondent groups, at the broader community or population levels. 6) Most studies fail to measure their programmes' medium- and long-term outcomes. 7) Few interventions examine the mechanism through which change occurs or the influence of related risk factors. 8) Finally, only very few studies examined the cost-effectiveness or the optimal intensity of their interventions concerning the desired outcomes.

Evidence gaps are in key areas

Most of the identified evidence gaps are observed in those areas where such evidence would be most needed and valuable. For example, the regions with the highest prevalence of VAWG (South Asia, Middle East and North Africa, and Sub-Saharan Africa) have some of the lowest rates of good quality impact assessment studies. Likewise, women and girls belonging to vulnerable groups are at the same time more likely to experience VAWG and less likely to be part of the targeted VAWG intervention programme. Furthermore, VAWG tends to be substantially higher in conflict and post-conflict populations, yet we know the least about what works in these contexts. Such a situation means that those women and girls who need help the most tend to get it the least and that we know very little, if anything at all, about how to help them effectively.

Evidence gaps are preventing the scaling of good practices

Most of the critical information needed to build upon positive evidence, scale it up, and adapt it for use in broader contexts is not available. For example, most programmes do not measure impact across more general population categories, do not measure longer-term effects and lack information on the potential scalability of any given intervention to other similar or distinct contexts. In addition, there is little solid evidence on the mechanism of intervention and the process through which desired change could be generated and sustained, as testified in the widespread instances of "conflicting" evidence among the programmes implementing similar strategies. Surveyed reviews also indicate a great deal of heterogeneity between study outcomes. These outcomes vary not only across different intervention strategies and types of VAWG but also across the studies that utilise the same approach and target the same form of violence. In other cases, the effects of a particular intervention are unclear, with some outcomes positively influenced and not the others. In such a situation, it is challenging to extract a consistent and reliable set of empirical insights on "what works" in this area that could be used to improve the effectiveness of new VAWG interventions.

Key lessons learned

Nonetheless, a small but growing body of rigorously tested interventions demonstrates that preventing VAWG is possible and can achieve large effect sizes. The interventions with the most positive findings used multiple, well-integrated approaches and engaged with numerous stakeholders over more extended periods. They also addressed underlying risk factors for violence, including social norms regarding gender dynamics and the acceptability of violence and women's economic independence. Surveyed findings also indicate the need to employ an approach adequate to the given situation, cultural and socio-economic context and to engage key local stakeholders to give them a sense of agency and ownership of the programme's goals.

Moving forward, identified limitations in the quantity and quality of empirical evidence on "what works" and limited effectiveness of the VAWG interventions, in general, all point to the imperative of significantly increasing investment in the rigorous impact evaluation of VAWG programmes. These investments should especially prioritise research conducted in the areas with identified evidence gaps, including studies conducted in the LMIC contexts, with vulnerable populations, and in conflict areas. Furthermore, evaluation studies with crucial design characteristics that enable the potential scalability of their results should be prioritised. These features include a more comprehensive target population, more extended impact tracking, examination of mechanisms of change and related broader risk factors, and consideration of the intervention's scalability, sustainability, and cost-effectiveness.

Prevention of VAWG is possible but not easy to achieve. VAWG programmes have to be designed with the required expertise and knowledge, building upon the best available evidence and fully accounting for the complexity of issues at hand. Importantly, they have to be accompanied by a robust impact assessment design to evaluate their effectiveness accurately. Generation of such evidence would help build a much-needed knowledge base on what works and what doesn't. This area badly needs such knowledge to improve the effectiveness of its interventions with the ultimate aim of preventing VAWG from occurring or helping its victims in moments of need.

Key resources

- ***What Works to Prevent Violence Against Women and Girls Global Programme*** is a UK-funded global program that has invested significant funds into program implementation and monitoring and evaluation work. The program resulted in a considerable amount of beneficial reports and tools, available at: https://www.whatworks.co.za/

- ***Interventions to Prevent or Reduce Violence Against Women and Girls***: A Systematic Review of Reviews – a World Bank report representing a meta-analysis of available evaluation studies in the VAWG area. Available at: http://hdl.handle.net/10986/21035

- UN Women's website on ***Ending VAWG*** (available at www.endvawnow.org) is a valuable website providing advice, including on M&E, divided by sectoral intervention.

- World Health Organisation - **RESPECT women: Preventing violence against women**, a framework to facilitate scaling up of evidence-informed strategies to prevent violence against women: www.who.int/reproductivehealth/publications/preventing-vaw-framework-policymakers/en/[1]

- ***The Reproductive Health Response in Conflict (RHRC)*** Consortium has developed a program M&E tool for VAWG in conflict-affected settings (available at: http://www.rhrc.org/resources/gbv/gbv_tools/manual_toc.html). Their training provides assessment tools, program design tools and M&E tools. The M&E section includes monitoring forms, an example of indicators to use

---

1. http://www.who.int/reproductivehealth/publications/preventing-vaw-framework-policymakers/en/

and references to other resources.

- The NGO *Raising Voices* has developed several practical, low-cost community-based approaches to measure the impact of Sasa!, their VAWG strategy (available at: http://www.raisingvoices.org/publications.php).
- **African GBV Prevention Network:** http://preventgbvafrica.org/understanding-vaw/vaw-resources/
- **Interagency Gender Working Group (IGWG):** http://www.igwg.org/
- **International Center for Research on Women (ICRW):** http://www.icrw.org/
- **Sexual Violence Research Initiative (South Africa):** http://www.svri.org/documents/svri-publications
- *The Gender-Equitable Men (GEM)* scale (available at http://www.popcouncil.org/Horizons/ORToolkit/AIDSQuest/instruments/gemscale.pdf) is a valuable resource to measuring the attitudes of men towards gender equality. The GEM scale has identified several attitudes associated with a decrease in VAWG.
- *The MEASURE Evaluation* (Bloom, S. S. (2008) *Violence against Women and Girls. A Compendium of Monitoring and Evaluation Indicators,* Chapel Hill, NC: Carolina Population Center) has produced a compendium of M&E indicators on VAWG (available at: http://www.cpc.unc.edu/measure/publications/pdf/ms-08-30.pdf). The report outlines good indicators to measure the magnitude and characteristics of VAWG, indicators relevant to programs according to the sector, and indicators for under-documented forms of VAWG, humanitarian settings and prevention programs.
- *Gender-Based Violence Information Management System (GBVIMS)*[2] aims to provide program managers with a

straightforward system to manage their data on reported GBV cases, including the safe and ethical sharing of reported incident data. Effective utilization of the GBVIMS can also assist service providers in understanding better the reported GBV cases they receive to: adjust their programming to more effectively respond to the needs of survivors; aggregate data to analyze broader trends and threats; enable safe sharing for improved inter-agency coordination and joint action to address emerging issues.

- ***The Committee on the Elimination of Discrimination against Women (CEDAW)***[3] is the body of independent experts monitoring the implementation of the Convention on the Elimination of All Forms of Discrimination against Women. The website provides information on the countries that have ratified the convention, the latest reports by country, and other valuable documents.

- ***The Due Diligence Project***[4] is a research-advocacy project that aims to add content to the international legal principle of "due diligence" in the context of State responsibility to end VAWG. The objective is to create an accountability framework based on the due diligence principle, namely the Due Diligence Framework, together with guiding principles that are concrete and measurable across regions. Heise, Lori; Ellsberg, Mary; Gottemoeller, Megan. (1999). Ending Violence Against Women. Population Reports, Series L. No. 11.

- ***The International Women's Rights Action Watch (IWRAW)***[5] was organized in 1985 at the Third World Conference on Women in Nairobi, Kenya. It aims to promote

---

2. *http://www.gbvims.com/gbvims-tools/*

3. *http://www.ohchr.org/en/hrbodies/cedaw/pages/cedawindex.aspx*

4. *http://www.duediligenceproject.org/*

5. *http://www1.umn.edu/humanrts/iwraw/*

recognition of women's human rights under the United Nations Convention on the Elimination of All Forms of Discrimination against Women (CEDAW), an international human rights treaty.

- ***The Stop Violence Against Women website (STOPVAW)***[6], a project of The Advocates for Human Rights, is a forum for information, advocacy, and change in promoting women's human rights worldwide.

- UNFPA. (2007). Ending Widespread Violence Against Women.

- UNFPA, UNIFEM, OSAGI. (2005). Combating Gender-Based Violence: A Key to Achieving the MDGS.

- United Nations General Assembly. (6 July 2006). An in-depth study on all forms of violence against women: Report of the Secretary-General. 61st session.

- UN Women. (2012). Handbook for National Action Plans on Violence Against Women. New York: UN Women.

- U.S. Agency for International Development (USAID). (2009). A Guide to Programming Gender-based Violence Prevention and Response Activities. Gender-Based Violence Working Group.

- WHO (World Health Organization). (2013). Global and regional estimates of violence against women: Prevalence and health effects of intimate partner violence and non-partner sexual violence. Geneva.

- ***Women's Refugee Commission***. (2011). Preventing Gender-based Violence, Building Livelihoods Guidance and Tools for Improved Programming[7].

---

6. *http://www.stopvaw.org/*

7. http://www.cpcnetwork.org/resource/preventing-gender-based-violence-building-livelihoodsguidance-and-tools-for-improved-programming/

References:

Arango, Diana & Morton, Matthew & Gennari, Floriza & Kiplesund, Sveinung & Ellsberg, Mary. (2014). Interventions to prevent or reduce violence against women and girls: A systematic review of reviews. http://dx.doi.org/10.13140/RG.2.1.2545.6168

Austrian, A., Muthengi, M. (2013). Safe and smart savings products for vulnerable adolescent girls in Kenya and Uganda. New York: Population Council.

Bandiera, O., Buehren, N., Burgess, R., Goldstein, M., Gulesci, S., Rasul, I., and Sulaiman, M. (2018). Women's Empowerment in Action: Evidence from a Randomized Control Trial in Africa. Washington, DC: World Bank.

Berg, R.C. & Denison, E. (2012).Interventions to reduce the prevalence of female genital mutilation/cutting in African countries. Campbell Systematic Review (9).

Blanchard, A., et al. (2013). Community mobilization, empowerment and HIV prevention among female sex workers in south India. BMC, 13, 234.

Bott, S., Morrison, A., & Ellsberg, M. (2005). Preventing and responding to gender-based violence in middle and low-income countries: A global review and analysis. Working Paper.

Breiding, M., et al. (2015). Intimate Partner Violence Surveillance: Uniform Definitions and Recommended Data Elements. Atlanta: Center for Disease Control and Prevention.

Coker, A. L., Bush, H. M., Cook-Craig, P. G., DeGue, S. A., Clear, E. R., Brancato, C. J., ... & Recktenwald, E. A. (2017). RCT testing bystander effectiveness to reduce violence. American Journal of Preventive Medicine, 52(5), 566-578.

Cork, C., White, R.G., Noel, P., Bergin, N. (2018). Randomised controlled trials of interventions addressing intimate partner violence in sub-Saharan Africa: A systematic review. Trauma, Violence, & Abuse https://doi.org/10.1177/1524838018784585

Crawford, S. with Lloyd-Laney, M., Bradley, T, Atherton, L., and Byrne, G. (2020). 'Final Performance Evaluation of DFID's What Works to Prevent Violence Against Women and Girls Programme', DFID's What Works to Prevent VAWG Programme, IMC Worldwide: Surrey.

DFID (2012). Guidance on Monitoring and Evaluation for Programming on Violence against Women and Girls. https://assets.publishing.service.gov.uk/government/uploads/system/uploads/attachment_data/file/67334/How-to-note-VAWG-3-monitoring-eval.pdf

Doyle, K., Levtov, R. G., Barker, G., Bastian, G. G., Bingenheimer, J. B., Kazimbaya, S., ... & Shattuck, D. (2018). Gender-transformative Bandebereho couples' intervention to promote male engagement in reproductive and maternal health and violence prevention in Rwanda:

Findings from a randomized controlled trial. PloS One, 13(4).

Duggan, A., McFarlane, E. C., Windham, A. M., Rohde, C. A., Salkever, D. S., &Fuddy, L. (1999). Evaluation of Hawaii's healthy start program. The Future of Children, 3(1): 66-90.

Dunkle et al. (2019). Impact of the Indashyikriwa training curriculum for couples on intimate partner violence in Rwanda: cluster randomized control trial. Draft manuscript – What Works.

Durlak, J. A., Weissberg, R. P., Dymnicki, A. B., Taylor, R. D., & Schellinger, K. B. (2011). The impact of enhancing students' social and emotional learning: a meta-analysis of school-based universal interventions. Child Development, 82(1), 405–432.

Ellsberg, Mary & Arango, Diana & Morton, Matthew & Gennari, Floriza & Kiplesund, Sveinung & Contreras, Manuel & Watts, Charlotte. (2014). Prevention of Violence against Women and Girls: What Does the Evidence Say?. The Lancet. http://dx.doi.org/10.1016/S0140-6736(14)61703-7

IRC. (2012). Getting down to business: Women's economic and social empowerment in Burundi. New York: International Rescue Committee.

Feder, L., Austin, S., & Wilson, D. (2008). Court Mandated Interventions for Individuals Convicted of Domestic Violence. Campbell Systematic Review (12).

Feinberg, M., Jones, D.E., Hostetler, M.L., Roettger, M.E., Paul, I.M., Ehrenthal, D.B. (2016). Couple-Focused Prevention at the Transition to Parenthood, a Randomized Trial: Effects on Coparenting, Parenting, Family Violence, and Parent and Child Adjustment, Prevention Science, 17(6), 751–764.

Fergus, L. (2012). Background paper for the UN Women Expert Group Meeting: Prevention of Violence Against Women and Girls in Bangkok, Thailand. Bangkok, Thailand: UN Women.

Florquin, Nicolas. (2016). Gender-Based Violence Interventions: Opportunities for Innovation. https://www.researchgate.net/publication/335335870_ Gender-Based_Violence_Interventions_Opportunities _for_Innovation

Gennari, Floriza. (2014). Violence Against Women and Girls Resource Guide.10.13140/RG.2.1.3811.1445. https://www.researchgate.net/publication/282980535_ Violence_Against_Women_and_Girls_Resource_Guide

Green, S., Prof, & Higgins, J. P. T. (Eds.).(2009). Cochrane handbook for systematic reviews of interventions. Hoboken, NJ: Wiley-Blackwell.

Green, E. P., Blattman, C., Jamison, J., & Annan, J. (2015). Women's entrepreneurship and intimate partner violence: A cluster randomized trial of microenterprise assistance and partner participation in post-conflict Uganda. Social Science & Medicine, 133, 177-188.

Gupta, J., Falb, K. L., Lehmann, H., Kpebo, D., Xuan, Z., Hossain, M., ... & Annan, J. (2013). Gender norms and economic empowerment intervention to reduce intimate partner violence against women in rural Côte d'Ivoire: A randomized controlled pilot study. BMC International Health & Human Rights, 13(1), 46.

Heise, L. (1998). Violence against women: An integrated, ecological framework. Violence Against Women, 4, 262-290.

Heise, L. (2011). What works to prevent partner violence? An evidence overview. Working Paper. STRIVE Research Consortium, London School of Hygiene and Tropical Medicine, London.

Heise L. (2012). Determinants of partner violence in low and middle-income countries: exploring variation in individual and population-level risk [PhD thesis]. London: London School of Hygiene & Tropical Medicine.

Hidrobo, M., Peterman, A., & Heise, L. (2016). The effect of cash, vouchers, and food transfers on intimate partner violence: Evidence from a randomized experiment in Northern Ecuador. American Economic Journal: Applied Economics, 8(3), 284-303.

Hossain, M., Zimmerman, C., Kiss, L., Abramsky, T., Kone, D., ... & Watts, C. (2014). Working with men to prevent intimate partner violence in a conflict-affected setting: a pilot cluster randomized controlled trial in rural Côte d'Ivoire. BMC Public Health, 14(1), 339-350.

Jewkes, R., Nduna, M., Levin, J., Jama, N., Dunkle, K., Puren, A., & Duvvury, N. (2008). Impact of stepping stones on incidence of HIV and HSV-2 and sexual behaviour in rural South Africa: Cluster randomised controlled trial. BMJ, 337, a506.

Karnataka Health Promotion Trust. (2012). Evaluation of Community Mobilization and Empowerment in relation to HIV Prevention among Female Sex Workers in Karnataka State, South India.

Kerr-Wilson, A.; Gibbs, A.; McAslan Fraser E.; Ramsoomar, L.; Parke, A.; Khuwaja, HMA.; and Jewkes, R. (2020). A rigorous global evidence review of interventions to prevent violence against women and girls, What Works to Prevent Violence Against Women and Girls Global Programme, Pretoria, South Africa. https://www.whatworks.co.za/documents/publications/ 374-evidence-reviewfweb/file

Kim, J., et al. (2009). Assessing the incremental effects of combining economic and health interventions: the IMAGE study in South Africa. WHO Bulletin, 87, 824-832.

Lee-Rife, S., Malhotra, A., Warner, A., & Glinksi, A. M. (2012). What Works to Prevent Child Marriage: A Review of the Evidence. Studies in Family Planning 43(4): 287-303.

Le Roux, E., Corboz, J., Scott, N., Sandilands, M., Baghuma Lele, U., Bezzolato, E., Jewkes, R. (2019). Engaging with faith groups to prevent VAWG in conflict-affected communities: results from two community surveys in the DRC. Draft manuscript – What Works

Lester, S., Lawrence, C., & Ward, C. L. (2017). What do we know about preventing school violence? A systematic review of systematic reviews. Psychology, Health & Medicine, 22(1), 187-223.

Livingston, M. (2008). A longitudinal analysis of alcohol outlet density and assault. Alcoholism: Clinical and Experimental Research, 32(6), 1074-1079.

Mathews, C., Eggers, S. M., Townsend, L., Aarø, L. E., de Vries, P. J., Mason-Jones, A. J., ... & Wubs, A. (2016). Effects of PREPARE, a multi-component, school-based HIV and intimate partner violence (IPV) prevention Programme on adolescent sexual risk behaviour and IPV: Cluster randomised controlled trial. AIDS and Behavior, 20(9), 1821-1840.

Mennicke, A., Kennedy, S. C., Gromer, J., & Klem-O'Connor, M. (2018). Evaluation of a social norms sexual violence prevention marketing campaign targeted toward college men: attitudes, beliefs, and behaviors over 5 years. Journal of Interpersonal Violence, 0886260518780411.

Michau, L., Horn, J., Bank, A., Dutt, M. & Zimmerman, C. (2015). Prevention of violence against women and girls: lessons from practice. Lancet, 385: 1672-1684,

Miller, E., et al. (2012). "Coaching boys into men": a cluster-randomized controlled trial of a dating violence prevention program. Adolescent Health, 51(5), 431-438.

Murray et al. (2019). Effectiveness of the Common Elements Treatment Approach (CETA) in reducing intimate partner violence and hazardous alcohol use in Zambia (VATU): a randomised controlled trial. Draft manuscript - What Works

Ogum-Alangea, D., Addo-Lartey, A., Chirwa, E., Sikweyiya, Y., Coker-Appiah, D., Jewkes, R., & Adanu, R. (2019). The Rural Response System Intervention to reduce Intimate Partner Violence in the Central Region of Ghana: Findings from a cluster-randomized controlled trial evaluation. Draft manuscript – What Works.

Pettifor, A., Lippman, S. A., Gottert, A., Suchindran, C. M., Selin, A., ... & Tollman, S. (2018). Community mobilization to modify harmful gender norms and reduce HIV risk: Results from a community cluster randomized trial in South Africa. Journal of the International AIDS Society, 21(7).

Picon, MG, Rankin, K, Ludwig, J, Sabet, SM, Delaney, A and Holst, A. (2017). Intimate partner violence prevention: an evidence gap map, 3ie Evidence Gap Map Report 8. International Initiative for Impact Evaluation (3ie). https://www.researchgate.net/publication/324840313_
Intimate_partner_violence_prevention_An_evidence_gap_map

Pronyk, P. M., Hargreaves, J. R., Kim, J. C., Morison, L. A., Phetla, G., Watts, C., ... & Porter, J. D. (2006). Effect of a structural intervention for the prevention of intimate-partner violence and HIV in rural South Africa: A cluster randomised trial. The Lancet, 368(9551), 1973-1983.

Pulerwitz, J., Hughes, L., Mehta, M., Kidanu, A., Verani, F., & Tewolde, S. (2015). Changing gender norms and reducing intimate partner violence: Results from a quasi-experimental intervention study with young men in Ethiopia. American Journal of Public Health, 105(1), 132-137.

Pundir P, Saran A, White H, Subrahmanian R, Adona J. (2020). Interventions for reducing violence against children in low- and middle-income countries: An evidence and gap map. Campbell Systematic Reviews, Vol. 16/4. https://doi.org/10.1002/cl2.1120

Ramsoomar, L., Ladbury, R. & Jewkes, R. (2021). Research uptake, lessons from a multi-country global programme: What Works to Prevent Violence against women and girls, Development in Practice. https://doi.org/10.1080/09614524.2021.1911952

Reza-Paul, S., et al. (2012). Sex worker-led structural interventions in India: a case study on addressing violence in HIV prevention through the Ashodaya Samithi collective in Mysore. Indian Journal of Medical Research. 135(1), 98–106.

Roy, S., Hidrobo, M., Hoddinott, J., & Ahmed, A. (2018). Transfers, behavior change communication, and intimate partner violence: Post-program evidence from rural Bangladesh. Review of Economics and Statistics, 1(0), 1-45.

Senn, C. Y., Eliasziw, M., Barata, P. C., Thurston, W. E., Newby-Clark, I. R., Radtke, H. L., & Hobden, K. L. (2015). Efficacy of a sexual assault resistance program for university women. New England Journal of Medicine, 372(24), 2326-2335.

Senn, C. Y., Eliasziw, M., Hobden, K. L., Newby-Clark, I. R., Barata, P. C., Radtke, H. L., & Thurston, W. E. (2017). Secondary and 2-year outcomes of a sexual assault resistance program for university women. Psychology of Women Quarterly, 41(2), 147-162.

Smedslund, G., Dalsbø, T. K., Sterio, A. K., Winsvold, A., & Clench-Aas, J. (2007).Cognitive behavioral therapy for men who physically abuse their female partner. Cochrane Database of Systematic Reviews (2).

Solotaroff, J., Pande, R. (2014). Violence Against Women and Girls: Lessons from South Asia. South Asia Development Forum. Washington: World Bank Publications

UNICEF, (2001). Commercial Sexual Exploitation and Sexual Abuse of Children in South Asia. Kathmandu: UNICEF Regional Office for South Asia.

USAID South Africa. (2013). Evaluation of Project Concern International. Washington: USAID.

Verma, R., et al. (2008). Promoting gender equity as a strategy to reduce HIV risk and gender-based violence among young men in India, in Horizons Final Report. Washington: Population Council.

World Health Organization, (1999). Report of the Consultation on Child Abuse Prevention. Geneva: World Health Organization.

World Health Organization, (2005). WHO multi-country study on women's health and domestic violence against women. Geneva: World Health Organization.

World Health Organization, (2013). Global and regional estimates of violence against women: prevalence and health effects of intimate partner violence and non-partner sexual violence. Geneva: World Health Organization. www.who.int/reproductivehealth[1].

World Health Organization, (2015). Violence against women; intimate partner violence and sexual violence. Geneva: World Health Organization. https://www.who.int/news-room/fact-sheets/detail/violence-against-women.

World Health Organization, (2018). Global Fact Sheet. Violence Against Women: Prevalence Estimates[2]

World Health Organization, (2019). RESPECT-Seven Strategies to Prevent Violence Against Women: Key Messages. https://apps.who.int/iris/bitstream/handle/10665/324967/WHO-RHR-19.11-eng.pdf.

Wolfe, D. et al. (2009). A school-based program to prevent adolescent dating violence: A cluster randomized trial. Archives of Pediatrics & Adolescent Medicine, 163(8), 692–699.

Zwi, K., Woolfenden, S., Wheeler, D. M., O'Brien, T., Tait, P., &Williams, K.J. (2007). School-based education

---

1. http://www.who.int/reproductivehealth

2. https://apps.who.int/iris/rest/bitstreams/1349966/retrieve

programmes for the prevention of child sexual abuse. Cochrane Database of Systematic Reviews (3).

[1] ~~Fulu and Kerr-Wilson (2015), for example, organise school-level curricular~~ changes relevant to IPV prevention as institutional-level interventions.

[2] SASA!

[3] Ref.

[4] See "Key terminology" section for explanations of experimental and quasi-experimental designs.

[5] The definitions of criteria are available at Kerr-Wilson et al, 2020, p. ii; details of programme evaluations are available in Kerr-Wilson et al, 2020, p 72-75.

[6] More about the campaign: https://www.alignplatform.org/resources/bell-bajao-campaign

[7] A Measurement Tool to Assess Systematic Reviews (AMSTAR) is a check list tool for appraising the quality of a systematic review. More details are available at: https://amstar.ca

[8] Such omission can result in inflated rates of statistically significant results just because with many examined effects some are bound to be statistically significant due to the chance alone, with the measured effect actually being null.

[9] An example of a meta-analysis of empirical evidence illustrating this principle of diminishing intervention impacts over time, see in Durlak and colleagues (2015).

Don't miss out!

Visit the website below and you can sign up to receive emails whenever Dr. Milos Kankaras publishes a new book. There's no charge and no obligation.

https://books2read.com/r/B-A-LEAZ-HFXZB

BOOKS 2 READ

Connecting independent readers to independent writers.

Did you love *Violence Against Women and Girls: Effectiveness of Intervention Programs*? Then you should read *Policy and Research on Gender Equality: An Overview*[3] by Milos Kankaras!

[4]

This book provides a brief and up-to-date overview of the global state of gender equality policy and research. In the first part, dealing primarily with policy, the book lists the main actors and stakeholders in the field and outlines the development of international legal and policy frameworks on gender equality and related issues. The book also introduces key frameworks and perspectives on gender equality and briefly discusses the main aspects and dimensions identified across various approaches. In the second part, dealing with empirical issues, the author examines the main sources of empirical evidence, international analytical studies and indicators, and data depositories on

3. https://books2read.com/u/mBzEYy

4. https://books2read.com/u/mBzEYy

gender equality. Finally, the book concludes with the chapter outlining key limitations and empirical data gaps in internationally available empirical evidence.

Also by Dr. Milos Kankaras

A Simple Guide

Lev Vygotsky's Theory of Cognitive Development: A Simple Guide

Gender Equality

Violence Against Women and Girls: Effectiveness of Intervention Programs

Domestic Violence: Effectiveness of Intervention Programs

Standalone

Jean Piaget's Theory of Cognitive Development: A Simple Guide

Watch for more at https://oecd.academia.edu/MilošKankaraš.

About the Author

Dr Miloš Kankaraš is an experienced policy analyst, project manager and author with a rich track record in providing an empirical foundation for evidence-based public policy in international settings. He worked in academia before moving to some of the leading international organisations, where he examined issues ranging from education, skill development, social policy, working conditions, gender equality, quality of life, etc. Miloš published extensively in a variety of policy and research areas. He has an undergraduate degree in Psychology, graduate degrees in educational psychology and international social policy, and a PhD in the area of cross-cultural research.